Praise for *Dancing on the Sun Stone*

"At the heart of *Dancing on the Sun Stone* is a daring and subversive juxtaposition. Becker sets several heretofore little-known Mexican women dancing in a church one evening in 1937 alongside one well-known literary giant, Octavio Paz. Through the eyes and experience of the women, we see Paz's poetics and politics anew. The result a luminous hybrid of history, memoir, literary analysis, gender studies, and penetrating political critique, written in a poet's lyrical prose."

—James Goodman, author of *But Where Is the Lamb? Imagining the Story of Abraham and Isaac*

"This unique and thought-provoking book is at once a marvelous social history of gender in revolutionary and post-revolutionary Mexico, an invitation to break down disciplinary barriers, and an autobiographical reflection of a great historian at work."

—Jürgen Buchenau, editor of *Mexico OtherWise: Modern Mexico in the Eyes of Foreign Observers*

"Marjorie Becker gives us a new language, historical and metaphorical, to reframe not only the history of Mexican women and girls, but also Mexican temporalities and the poetry of Octavio Paz. A creative mixed-genre experiment, this important book blends historical analysis, poetics of history, and memoir. The result is a bold, deeply original, and beautifully written work. This book will engage many kinds of readers: historians, literary scholars, and anyone seeking fresh insight on women's voices in history."

—Steve J. Stern, author of *The Secret History of Gender: Women, Men, and Power in Late Colonial Mexico*

"This concise volume, beautifully crafted by a distinguished historian of Mexico who is also a well-published poet, provides a unique perspective on gender relations and politics in modern Mexico. The product of years of archival research and rich oral histories with generations of Michoacan women, and structured as a sustained engagement on Mexican identity with the late Nobel-prizewinning poet Octavio Paz, *Dancing on the Sun Stone* provides a fresh and timely appreciation of the gendered dynamics of modern Mexican life. Imaginatively straddling literary genres and academic disciplines, Becker's volume deserves a place in both scholarly libraries and the undergraduate classroom."

—Gilbert M. Joseph, Farnam Professor Emeritus of History and International Studies, Yale University, and co-editor (with Tim Henderson) of *The Mexico Reader: History, Culture, Politics*

DANCING ON THE SUN STONE

Marjorie Becker

DANCING

on the

SUN STONE

Mexican Women
and the Gendered Politics
of Octavio Paz

UNIVERSITY OF NEW MEXICO PRESS / ALBUQUERQUE

ISBN 978-0-8263-6418-0 (cloth)
ISBN 978-0-8263-6419-7 (e-book)

Library of Congress Control Number: 2022947680

Founded in 1889, the University of New Mexico sits on the traditional homelands of the Pueblo of Sandia. The original peoples of New Mexico—Pueblo, Navajo, and Apache—since time immemorial have deep connections to the land and have made significant contributions to the broader community statewide. We honor the land itself and those who remain stewards of this land throughout the generations and also acknowledge our committed relationship to Indigenous peoples. We gratefully recognize our history.

COVER ILLUSTRATION *Sun Stone* Mindy Basinger Hill
Dancer Ioan Florin Cnejevici | istockphoto.com

DESIGNED BY Mindy Basinger Hill

COMPOSED IN 11 /14.5 pt Adobe Jenson Pro, Calluna Sans

CONTENTS

ACKNOWLEDGMENTS

It is a tremendous pleasure to acknowledge the people who, through their kindness, comprehension, and grace, have accompanied me on the journeys prompting *Dancing on the Sun Stone*. My parents, the late Carrie Popper Becker and the late Marvin Jerome ("Buddy") Becker, were incomparable. Their dedication to the world's possibilities for magnitude and beneficence, their concern for a vast array of individuals, their utter dedication to their family, emerged through so many of their gestures. I also cannot say enough about my sister, Joan Becker; and my brother, Simon Becker, and his wife, Lisa Becker, for their unerring thoughtfulness.

A number of my formal teachers are also extraordinary individuals who, through listening to and reading my ideas, my chapters, my creative work, and through sharing their own perspectives and views, have proved incomparable. Most especially, Florencia Mallon and Steve J. Stern have long accompanied me and through the keenness of their empathy, the range of their kindness, have helped me use—rather than deny—the intensity informing my approaches to Latin America. I have long been tremendously grateful to them for accepting my request to create an independent study focusing on modern Mexican history when they taught me in grad school at Yale. I am yet more grateful for the friendship we have shared ever since.

This project possesses many births. If in my introduction I invite readers into the realms of my approaches, it is much because of the significance of Michoacanos, of history and of poetry. Certainly, I was fortunate enough first to encounter Octavio Paz's "Sun Stone" in Dr. John Fein's Latin American literature class at Duke. And in fact, I was fortunate enough to attend Duke as an undergraduate, and to later initiate my profession as Latin American historian in history grad school there. There I studied with a number of inspirational teachers including the late Anne F. Scott from whom I began to learn US women's history while I also participated in the women's group that influenced my feminism. They included the late Reynolds Price and the late Helen Bevington, who provided arenas for my experiments in creative writing. They certainly include the late Larry Goodwyn whose courses in southern history and in oral history enabled me to ponder the world and my own future in new, inviting ways.

My experiences in graduate school at Duke, and then at Yale, have been part of an intellectual mosaic as both schools prompted me to develop the world view I maintain, one centering on the doings of the often unseen. The professors at Duke who helped me even to consider developing a perspective include Goodwyn, the remarkable Latin Americanist professors including the deeply missed late Chuck Bergquist, the late John Tepaske, and Arturo Valenzuela. Then, at Yale, I was fortunate enough to study with other amazing professors. My advisor there, Emilia Viotti da Costa, demonstrated an insightful understanding of the worlds of the Latin American populations and their historical engagements and travails. I also was fortunate enough to study nineteenth century Mexican history with Silvia Arrom. Not only is her own work on Mexican women crucial, but I also will never forget how carefully and kindly she taught Mexican history. At Yale, too, I studied labor history with the late David Montgomery and US women's history with Nancy Cott. There, too, I met James C. Scott, the compelling political scientist of the peasantry with whom I was fortunate enough to discuss my initial findings focusing on rural Michoacán.

If, as a student, I read, thought, wrote, and wondered, it was in Mexico itself that I gained a sense of the worlds where the dancers and Paz lived, assessed, and, in the case of the dancers, remade. I am profoundly grateful to a number of people there whose kindness and insight were profound. They include Lila Toledo and her family. They include Beatrice Rojas and Jean Meyer, who I met in Zamora and who showered me with kindness there and in Mexico City. I will never forget our conversations about Cristeros, about Catholicism and Judaism, about (as Jean reminded me later), my hope to continue writing poetry. I also was lucky enough to meet Armida de la Vara and Luis González y González, Carlos Herrejón, Martín Sánchez, and Veronica Oikion.

An array of astonishing friends and colleagues have enhanced my experiences in Mexico, at conferences throughout the world, and in Los Angeles. I never forget my wonderful Mexican research friends, Becky Horn and Velma

García. I am extremely grateful to the remarkable scholars Barbara Weinstein, Brooke Larson, Claudio Lomnitz, and the late Friedrich Katz. I am also very grateful for the friendship of Peter Guardino and Jane Walter, Arnulfo Embríz, Robin King, Anne Rubinstein, Ana Miniam, Elizabeth Schwaller, José Moya, Amy Richlin, and Jim Krippner. Alex Aviña is a remarkable scholar and individual whom I count myself very fortunate to have trained in USC graduate school. Mexican history and historiography would not be what they are without the intellect, collegiality, and depth of kindness of Gil Joseph. I will never forget the pleasure of working with him and the late Daniel Nugent on the *Everyday Forms of State Formation* project. Robert Rosenstone and Jim Goodman are exceptional scholars and writers who played enormous roles in making *Rethinking History* the innovative journal that it is and have helped make it such a welcoming venue for creative work.

An array of granting agencies supported the research for my previous monograph, *Setting the Virgin on Fire*. While a number of physical and sexual assaults on my person prohibited my return to Mexico, I have found myself able to return to much of the documentation I discovered in multiple Mexican archives (some of which I was fortunate enough myself to discover) and, considering the information from a distinct perspective, use it anew. I am very grateful to the institutions that awarded me a Faculty Fulbright Research Fellowship for Mexico, a summer stipend from the American Council of Learned Societies and from the National Endowment for the Humanities; and awards from the American Association of University Women, from the Woodrow Wilson Foundation, from the Center for U.S. Mexican Studies, from Yale University, from the Hewlett Foundation, and from the History Department of the University of Southern California.

At the University of Southern California (USC), I am deeply grateful to the History Department staff, most particularly Lori Rogers, without whom the department simply would not run as it should. I am also grateful to Sandra Hopwood and Simone Bessant for the ways they help make the department such an inviting, well-run place. I am grateful to my colleagues for their appreciation of Latin American history and literature. In particular, I am immensely grateful to Gordon Berger, a model of friendship and compassion; to Terry Seip, to Paul Lerner, to the late Maria Elena Martínez, to Ayse Rorlich, Sarah Gaultieri; to Ramzi Rouighi, Alice Echols, Wolf Gruner, Josh Goldstein, Brett Sheehan, Joan Piggott, Edgardo Pérez Morales, George Sánchez,

Jason Glenn, Lon Kurashige, Deb Harkness, and Karen Halttunen. I am immensely grateful to Elinor Accampo and the classicist Carolyn Dewald, who were my first friends at USC. Carole Shammas has been a remarkable colleague whose support for Latin American history and whose sensitivity to creative work has proved unforgettable. I am so grateful to her for serving as my mentor. Various History Department chairs have supported this project; I am very grateful to Steve Ross, Peter Mancall, Bill Deverell, Phil Ethington, and Jay Rubenstein for their consistent backing.

Poetry returned to my life in Los Angeles many years ago. Building on the daily writing practice I established when I wrote *Setting the Virgin on Fire*, I became part of an enthralling poetry community; for many years this community became one of my USC colleague, friend, and mentor David St. John's weekly master classes. David himself has proved to be an astonishing mentor, a brilliant and kindhearted scholar. I cannot overstate how grateful I am to him for reading what I write as historian and as poet and for the attention he provided to my impassioned thinking about the dancers and poetry, and for spending time to read multiple versions of *Dancing on the Sun Stone*.

An array of beloved friends and relatives from my time in Macon and in poetry communities also accompanied me on this journey. They include Suzanne Cassidy, Alice Bullington Davis, Diana Figueroa, Roy Pattishall, the late Marian and Gus Kaufman, and the late Bill Maynard. They include, too, Dorothy Barresi, Marsha de la O, Judith Pacht, Candace Pearson, Cathie Sandstron, Lynne Thompson, Phil Taggart, Carine Topal, Jan Wesley, Gail Wronsky, and Brenda Yates.

I am deeply grateful to Michael Millman, the editor at the University of New Mexico Press who demonstrated such a helpful and kind approach to the acceptance of this book for publication. I can't overstate my gratitude to Jurgen Buchenau for introducing me to the Press's editors. I am also particularly grateful to Alexandra Hoff and James Ayers for their kind editorial assistance. I very much appreciate the thoughtful comments provided by readers Gil Joseph and Mary Kay Vaughan. I am especially grateful for their support for the approach I devised here, an approach based on my hope to behave democratically with my readers by sharing crucial sources of my thinking, feeling, experiences about the previously unseen and unheard gendered voices within a context of Mexican time. Needless to say, any errors of fact or interpretation in this multi-genre hyphenate of a book are my own.

The women who so captured my attention were not trained to dance in the church. They were not expected to seize and inhabit time as they did. They certainly did not expect to alter history. Their courage and spontaneity have never failed to impress me. That I was fortunate enough to meet one of them and to learn about all of them in Michoacán has long astonished me. I am overwhelmed by the fact that I have been allowed to consider both the weight and the contributions of the dancers' historical and literary experiences; to see the ways their lives, their experiences, their dance communicated such a beguiling historical and poetic language. And to recognize the ways that what they did not only made them participants in the grassroots movement prompted by Mexican president Lázaro Cárdenas and his efforts to change their circumstances during his 1934–1940 presidency, but also spoke in subtle and impassioned ways to people like Octavio Paz who failed to seek out and encounter those Michoacán women whose dance emerged as a dance on the Sun Stone.

DANCING ON THE SUN STONE

INTRODUCTION

One night in 1937, a group of women in the Mexican village of Ario Santa Monica, Michoacán, entered a church and enacted a powerful statement of their temporal range and reach by dancing. During research I undertook in Michoacán, the dancers and their critics entrusted me with their histories—histories that otherwise seemed unlikely to see the light of day. In part, this remarkable event became hidden because the dance took place within a conservative Catholic region where women learned they were to display modesty and subservience to men. In part, it was lost from view because the women lived at a time when Mexican women lacked equality before the law; in part, it survived only in obscurity because their neighbors understood the dance as an act of heresy and reviled the dancers.

Nonetheless, the dance in my view was an act of something far more historically significant than misbehavior. That night in the church, the dancers spoke with their bodies in response to constraints long imposed on their use of time, their education, and their psyches. Today, their courageous declarations invite us to amplify their voices, to hear what they said about gender, about revolution, about human temporal possibilities in modern Mexico.

Because of the women's complex use of time, because of their knowledge about and experiences of gender relations in modern Mexico, and because of their bravery in taking action, I believe it is important that their voices be heard more fully in the narrative of that history. One useful, if unconventional, means of achieving that goal is to place the dancers in dialogue with the ideas of Octavio Paz, Mexico's Nobel Prize–winning poet, cultural theorist, diplomat, and critic of assaults on popular aspirations for a democratic social order.[1]

During his illustrious life, Paz's voice was amplified within a wide variety of venues, but nowhere more eloquently than in his signature 1957 poem, "Sun Stone."[2] In that poem, the speaker Paz invites the reader to enter an emotional landscape filled with vibrant, erotically charged flowers, plants, and foodstuffs. Within this world, the reader is allowed to follow the speaker through his journey marked by sensual memories, experiences, and emotional quests as a Mexican man.

Initially, however, the journey is an anxious one, as Paz has created a speaker entrapped within his understanding of ancient Aztec time. For Paz, within Aztec cosmology, the sun stone marked time as a killing stone on which people were sacrificed, their blood used to enable the world to persist. For Paz and his speaker, Mexican time entrapped people, taking on a deeply authoritarian cast. People survived, but without spontaneity, living lives without meaning, experiencing each day as a repetition of the one before.

Paz uses the page as a landscape upon which he as Godlike creator populates the space with the narrator and many other people, particularly women. He includes within the poem's circular framework a history of the West from a Mexican perspective—a history filled with war, murder, lists of victims; it is a microhistory that can be read as an essay about the exhaustion of days, experienced by people lacking all emotion except despair at life's seeming emptiness.

Yet in contrast to the lifelessness, Paz leads the reader to a central verse set in Madrid in 1937 during the Spanish Civil War. There, in the midst of the bloodshed, he places a man and a woman taking off their clothes and making love. Observing this act alters Paz's speaker. It further changes the world itself, enabling him to understand time differently and to claim that time becomes significant only when people share food and water, thoughts and experiences, allowing individual men (though not women) to shed individuality and emerge fully able to experience life.

There is no small irony to the fact that it was Paz who, in his expressed hope for a more inclusive Mexico, utilized an overly rational approach, one enabling him to fail to consider the women who, themselves physical victims and survivors of the very authoritarian governments he critiques, devise a far more fluid, multihued, multifaceted series of perspectives. Indeed, accustomed to undertaking the most unappreciated array of Mexican tasks, they created a highly tinted, complex, sometimes contradictory approach. The women's behavior and, most especially, their dance can be understood as a blueprint for a different Mexico.

Until now, the vast and useful literature on Paz, a literature that has at times considered his interest in surrealism and at times analyzed his political turn from the far left to his concern about Mexican democracy, has ignored the Mexican dancers.[3] At the same time, the sophisticated historiography about revolution and gender has failed to assess Paz's poetics either for their complex artistry or as evidence illuminating Mexico's gendered history.[4] Indeed, no Mexican historian of whom I am aware has linked poetry's attention to emotionality and interiority with an interest in the cultural dimensions of Mexican power relations. Nonetheless, Paz's "Sun Stone" and the Michoacán dancers use time as a means to allow them to reveal their perspectives on Mexican gender relations and institutions, and the fact that they communicated their concerns quite independently from one another suggests that the field of Mexican cultural history can benefit deeply from a study assessing their complex approaches to Mexican time, gender, and history.

Because this project brings together and seeks to construct a particular bridge between two forms of perception—the historical approach concerned with cultures of temporal power relations, and a poetic approach sensitive to expressions of emotional life—it seems important to invite readers to consider my personal involvement with the women and men who entrusted their histories to me, alongside my long engagements with history and literature. How did I, a young historian enthralled by literature, move into more impassioned approaches to history, then into poetry itself? What, about my intellectual path, my own dance, prompted this project? Let me invite you to enter this dance, to dance with me.[5]

Born and raised Reform Jewish in Macon, Georgia, I grew up in a small city where neighborhoods dense with scent and color, wide and broad lawns graced by magnolia, azalea, camellia, and streams lined with daffodils, were owned by Macon's white elite. Yet nearby, unpaved red-clay roads led to the homes of the Black men and women who worked as servants for many white people. A few miles away there were commercial agricultural peach farms owned and managed by white people and worked by poorly paid Black people. If peaches and pecans, tomatoes and okra flourished, they did so much because of that outdoor work in dense humidity and 100-degree heat.

For me, despite doting relatives who wanted only the best for me, classism, sexism, and mild anti-Semitism played important roles in my earliest experiences. Somehow, too, when I was quite young, I noticed something about the unfairness of a system where Black women—many of whom had been extremely kind to me—were forced, after long days cleaning white people's homes, to wait at the end of the streets for buses that would take them home to their families. Once I went to grammar school, I sometimes heard school-mates' cruel and derogatory language about people I knew; somehow, despite my timidity, I tried to protect a Black woman who had treated me kindly against the verbal cruelty of a classroom bully. Though I didn't know this then, these observations and experiences would later prompt my attempts to write a sort of history about people whose worlds largely went unseen or misjudged.

Alongside Macon's (and more broadly, the Deep South's) consistent refusal to develop a public-school system dedicated to educating all children equally and well, in the late 1950s a new approach to language training emerged in Macon. That is, in a city almost entirely devoid of native Spanish speakers, a Puerto Rican woman arrived and persuaded the local board of education to allow her to establish and direct a Spanish-language immersion program in three of the public grammar schools. Because I attended one of those schools, I began learning Spanish as a child.

As unusual and progressive as this approach to schooling was, it is also true that Macon's public-school system then was almost completely segre-gated by gender and race. These facts were treated by the people I knew as though they did not exist and as though they had nothing at all to do with what we learned in school. Within that context, I found myself deeply drawn to history courses suggestive of other worlds, other people, English classes where as students we were taught to understand fictional worlds to be as tangible as our daily lives, to reenact—right there on the classroom floor—Shakespearean witches and their brews.

It was an environment that also somehow urged me, as the speeches I gave when I was confirmed at Temple Beth Israel and later when I was elected salutatorian of my high school class, to consider some of the forms of ra-cial injustice that had characterized Macon life—and some of the ways that white lives there had been enhanced by the generosity of Black people. On reflection, both the intimacy that existed in my life between specific Black people—Anne Matthews, the Black woman who worked as a cook for my grandparents and who weekly offered the shy child I was friendship and comfort; Annie Lizzie Howard, the practical nurse my mother sometimes hired to babysit—come to mind.

If before college I found myself interested in many topics and approaches, my undergraduate experiences at Duke University and the University of Madrid intensified that array of interests. This was much because I studied with remarkable professors. They included the late novelist Reynolds Price for whom I wrote a series of interrelated short stories; the poet Helen Bevington, who taught poetry composition; the remarkable professor of US women's history, Anne Firor Scott; and Larry Goodwyn, the astonishing professor of southern and oral history.

An enthralling classroom presence, Goodwyn lured me ever more deeply into the worlds of the racialized and class-bound South, a world I surely recognized. Most importantly, in his analysis of some of the sources of injustice I had experienced, Goodwyn emerged as the first person I knew who discussed and critiqued that world. Further, he noticed something about my intensity, my passion to hear and understand the history he communicated. Inviting me as an undergrad to enroll in his graduate oral-history class, he also volunteered to direct my honors thesis.

The thesis emerged as an assessment of the historical and psychological worlds informing Katharine Du Pre Lumpkin's autobiographical *The Making of a Southerner*.[6] A memoir informed by her personal perspective as the great-granddaughter of a slave-owner, *The Making* traces Lumpkin's emerging recognition of the dehumanization of Black people in her great-grandfather's time and in her own. It also discussed some of her own 1920s efforts to combat aspects of southern racism. What struck me about her book was its candor, its attempt to understand the connections between familial and social life in the Jim Crow South. Indeed, my classes with Scott and Goodwyn, and the project itself, prompted me to read an array of historical studies and novels focusing on race and gender.

Central to that project and to my training in oral history was an interview with Lumpkin, for which I took a Greyhound bus to Charlottesville where she lived. Meeting me at the station, taking me home for lunch, she emerged as the very "living source" so crucial to oral history. In retrospect, it strikes me that both the interview and her memoir sensitized me to what became the central theme of my thesis: the fact that her combined experiences of southern racism and sexism affected her in stirring ways. In particular, I came to believe that her experience of profiting daily from the fact that she was white, not Black, while also learning the ways that her gender worked against her in that misogynist culture, came to shape her political sensibility. Certainly, that recognition emerged as the crucial theme in my honors study, "Lumpkin's South."

As fascinated as I was by a sort of historical approach that privileges the research and assessment of individuals who had previously gone unsung, I also remained enthralled by classes in creative writing and those focusing on modern Spanish literature. Thus, at the point of graduation, I found myself uncertain about what to do next. What roles could my interests play in my future? Remarkably, Goodwyn noticed something about my concern and suggested I develop what he called a "ten-year-plan," allowing me to explore the worlds I found so intriguing.

In cobbling together such a plan, I initially accepted a friend's invitation to follow him to Bloomington, Indiana, where he was to attend graduate school. Though it may sound hopelessly ignorant and idealistic, perhaps even boastful, my plan was to use that time to establish a daily writing practice funded by menial work. That is, recognizing that my parents' support had protected me from the sort of jobs many people have been compelled to do, I found it important to see if I had the skills such work required.

In Bloomington, then, I began writing daily. I also found an array of low-paying jobs, including domestic work as a maid for a belly dancer. Jobs showing me something of the economic, physical, and psychological challenges of such work, they were also jobs that prompted me to seek work more consistent with my interests.[7] Determined to pursue other parts of my ten-year-plan, on a snowy Bloomington day, I drove to the Peace Corps office in Indianapolis. When I mentioned my Spanish-language skills, the Peace Corps officials offered me the chance to serve as a nutritionist working for the Paraguayan Ministry of Agriculture.

More precisely, what I received was an opportunity to begin thinking about the needs of the people who lived in that small, landlocked, Guaraní-speaking country. Indeed, the experience of living and working in the village of General Aquino provided all sorts of lessons: what it was to live (as most villagers did) with no electricity, no running water, no religious and scant educational institutions; what it was to live in a place where the daily temperature rose to 110 degrees for most of the year.

A key attraction of General Aquino was its deep personalism, the fashion in which my neighbors and the students I attempted to teach nutrition, basic first aid, gardening, and—at their request—embroidery, revealed themselves to me, and the ways they came to learn about me. I will certainly never forget the ways a group of Paraguayan women—wives of village merchants—befriended me. Though I never mentioned this to them, I had come to find my experiences living alone perplexing and frightening when, night after night, one of an array of unknown men arrived at my door erroneously believing that as a foreign woman living away from family, I invited them to take advantage of me. Visiting the women in their husband's general stores, I found myself in havens where over hours of gossip and *tereré*, the women took me in protectively.

My Peace Corps job itself provided me with an array of professional challenges. They ranged from traveling to villages even smaller than the one in which I lived to meet the girls and women with whom I would work, to persuading them to join the nutrition clubs I developed, to practicing soy-based recipes over a two-burner stove, to experimenting with the qualities of soil and fertilizer in order to teach gardening, to devising transportation—either walking or, ultimately, purchasing a horse and cart—when the Paraguayan Ministry of Agriculture truck failed.

Throughout, I wondered whether first my Spanish and then my Guaraní were expressive enough; my diligence in training people to eat more fruits, more vegetables, more soy, effective enough; my suggestions to remove sharp objects on the ground to protect their children helpful enough.[8] At the same time, being there provided me with incomparable opportunities to learn something of the physical and cultural workings of that part of South America. It is also true that during my time there, I wrote a draft of a novel, and I began considering ways to combine my Latin American experiences with imaginative writing.[9]

After traveling to Argentina, Brazil, Bolivia, and Peru, I returned to Macon and to the journalism work I had explored in high school and college. I was fortunate enough to receive a series of journalism jobs at the *Macon News* and the Associated Press. It was there as copy editor, and then as reporter, that I entered the worlds of hot type, of composing room bosses translating editors' marked-up pages. It was a world filled with typewriters, then computers the size of living rooms. And in that particular world in which I covered courts, education, health, the changing culture, I found myself in courthouses, law offices, even outside the prison cell housing the prisoner who had invited me for an interview. It was, in fact, a memorable job, allowing me to work with dedicated editors and fellow reporters; it was work I deeply loved.

If I left journalism and Macon for various reasons, I mainly left because the persistence of Macon racism and sexism felt undermining. It is also true that I had promised myself in Paraguay both to become a creative writer and to write a book about radical southern women. Believing I could write such a book in graduate school, I turned to Larry Goodwyn for advice.

In his response, Goodwyn invited me to come to graduate school at Duke, planning not to write a book that nestled comfortably within a settled tradition, but rather a book that would "radically alter that tradition."[10] Captivated by his encouragement, I entered Duke graduate school in history hoping to find documentation about women as innovative and brave as the southern women I knew. That this project never took shape was because I took Chuck Bergquist's graduate seminar in modern Latin American history.

A course enabling students to study central themes in modern Latin American history through the lens of countries' export economies, the wonder of the class resided in Professor Bergquist's passionate responses to his experiences serving in the Peace Corps in Colombia and his sensitivity to the ways my own Peace Corps experiences had affected me. Further, if the atmospheres of many approaches to professional history long had been and still consist of an array of unspoken male-dominated demands and gestures—this dinner party, that conference, this formal writing style eliminating a universe of sentiment and perspective—in Bergquist's seminar a different sensibility settled in, one alert to some of the music, the hues, even the hungry desperation alive in Latin America. Week by week, Bergquist's welcoming atmosphere enabled me to draw on and think about my passionate responses to Latin America.

Without doubt, it was Bergquist's sensitivities to my intellectual concerns and his belief in my intellect and drive that led me to devise a research project linking Octavio Paz's poetry and his cultural studies with the expansive historiography of the Mexican revolution of 1910. The project was ambitious not simply because it hoped to link history with poetry. It was also ambitious because at that point, I knew so little about Mexico, its great revolution, or Paz's work.

Still, when I first read "Sun Stone" in a literature class, I found the poem's sensual approaches to Mexican history compelling. Then, too, the summer after my sophomore year in college, my family had taken part in the Experiment in International Living, a program that enabled us to host Lila Toledo, a college student from Mexico City. An engaging woman just my age, Lila and her family became lifelong friends with me and my family. But that leaps ahead. In fact, at the goodbye party my family gave for the program participants, some of the students began playing records. As we danced and danced, I began to sense how intriguing it might be to study Mexico.

As for my initial understanding of Mexico's revolution of 1910, the crucial series of modern Mexican events that forever altered Mexico and indeed, the topic which would prove central to my work as a professional historian, that understanding was initially characterized by my left-leaning sense that a revolution made to undermine poverty and suffering must have emerged from deeply humane desires to better the world. That is, I found myself eager to study and write about a long, transformative series of national and international events, and to begin to understand those histories in relationship to Paz's work.

In the event, the research and writing I did for that project entitled "The Revolution and the Pyramid: A Critique of Octavio Paz" fascinated me. The paper itself prompted Bergquist to suggest that I become a historian of Latin America, rather than the US historian and writer I initially planned to become. Completing my masters at Duke, I entered the doctoral program in history at Yale in order to work with scholars who focused widely on colonial and modern Latin American history and specifically on Mexico and gender studies. There I studied Latin America's complex history, particularly its histories of the peasantry, ever more deeply. Expanding my focus on the Mexican revolution and its subsequent 1926–1929 popular religious counter-revolution, I continued to wonder why that revolution appeared to have so persistently ignored women.[11]

It would be the grassroots research I conducted in Mexico that enabled me to respond to that concern. Indeed, it was there in rural Mexico that I would discover the dancers and the dance. They were part of what I came to understand as a grassroots movement responding to Mexican President Lázaro Cárdenas's programmatic efforts to transform the Mexican countryside and its people. That program included an expansive land redistribution, a "socialist" approach to rural education through which teachers attempted to alter rural sensibilities, an array of anticlerical gestures seeking to undo the political influence of the Catholic Church, and women's leagues that, while not promoting gender equality, nonetheless, were to prove provocative.

My dissertation research enabled me to unearth the material cultural roots of Cárdenas's effort to govern his home state of Michoacán between 1928 and 1932. By focusing on the historical worlds of multiple Michoacanos, individuals previously ignored or denigrated, and by focusing on the socioeconomic structure of Cárdenas's government, I learned that, notwithstanding his popularity, the government Cárdenas developed proved to be hierarchical. Indeed, I found that the institutions he and his followers developed in Michoacán during his governorship served as a model for those established during his 1934–1940 presidency of Mexico.[12]

Often, history graduate students follow a relatively straightforward path, one that involves developing a dissertation topic for which there are ample written documents to assess, traveling to the archives where the documents are housed, conducting research, writing their dissertation, and responding to their advisors' advice about revision. In my case, the ramshackle, partly censored state of important Mexican archives, my hope to understand the Michoacán campesinos even more deeply, led me to apply for and receive a number of fellowships, including a Faculty Fulbright research fellowship enabling me to conduct additional research in Mexico City and throughout Michoacán.

During one such research trip in the village of Ario de Rayón, a stranger pursued me to tell me what he knew about a long-ago dance in Ario.[13] While initially I found what he said about the dance and its participants questionable, as I deepened my documentary and oral historical research, I also found myself hoping to understand Mexican history through a yet more empathic historical lens. That research revealed that numerous Michoacanos responded to Cárdenas's efforts to change their lives in complex ways during his presidency; that they had in fact developed a grassroots resistance movement compelling enough to alter elements of Mexico's postrevolutionary government.

It was a movement composed of many strands as the men and women who were the supposed beneficiaries of the Cardenista movement responded to its multiple efforts to change them in as many ways. While I had discussed some of the problems with Cárdenas's remarkable yet sadly inadequate approach established in Michoacán in my dissertation,[14] the research I conducted for what would emerge as a book quite unlike the dissertation showed some of the ways that northwestern Michoacán's startling physical beauty could not mask the practices of prerevolutionary, revolutionary, and, most especially, postrevolutionary injustice there.

While the Michocanos' uprising contained multiple, contradictory elements, it did so precisely because the rural population itself proved to be so complicated. Indeed, it was that very cultural complexity that had proved confusing to Cárdenas and to his followers; only through revealing their responses to Cardenista efforts to alter economy, schooling, daily habits, and indigenous roles and rights were the campesinos able to communicate elements of their own perspectives. And to me, perhaps the most remarkable responses to Cárdenas's approach were those of the women—those determined to maintain the conservative Catholic order over which the patron saint La Purísima and the wealthy women presided, and, most especially, those women also enamored of La Purísima—who invaded the church and danced. It was they who spoke to me in ever more enduring ways.

Before writing the book that I hoped would bring these complex rural peoples, their movement, their concerns, even their worlds to life, I discussed my findings with my mentor Florencia Mallon, an insightful scholar-teacher who had observed my work ethic, my forms of thinking, feeling, and writing. When I told her what I had discovered in Michoacán and what I believed my research meant, she mentioned that in her view, metaphor most clearly reflects my thought. Further, she suggested an approach I would come to know as one that creative writers sometimes employ. "Write it from your subconscious," she advised.

Through suggesting this unorthodox approach to writing history, Mallon prompted me to draw ever more deeply upon my compassion for my subjects, my sensitivity toward the individuals about whom I would write. But really. "Write from the subconscious." How do people do such a thing? In my case, in order to link the extensive body of information I had discovered with my inner forms of perception, I began each day to reread and memorize the information on the note cards relevant to the portion of the book I planned to write that day.[15] Then I walked through my neighborhood, pen and clean note cards in tow. Whenever ideas found their ways through my consciousness, I stopped to sit on whatever neighbor's lawn, on whatever patch of sidewalk, to write them down. Thus, in a fashion that may seem as haphazard as it was driven, I wrote the draft of what became the monograph entitled *Setting the Virgin on Fire: Lázaro Cárdenas, Michoacán Peasants, and the Redemption of the Mexican Revolution.*

In many respects, this experience was intriguing as it allowed me to build on extensive worlds I had discovered through many trips into unknown, ill-considered parts of the Mexican countryside. It enabled me to write about Mexican peasants, including the dancers, people who had used their bodies, minds, and sensibilities to make Mexico into what they considered a more just country. Assuredly, writing about those individuals in this physical way enabled me to develop my historical voice. At the same time, the unconventionality of my approach coupled with the fact that I was one of my university's few scholars focusing on Latin America and my department's only untenured faculty member proved unnerving until, to my happy surprise, I received book-contract offers from Cambridge University Press, Duke University Press, the University of California Press, University of Wisconsin Press, and Yale University Press, prompting my department to offer me tenure and promotion.[16]

Perhaps because of my longstanding focus on Mexican culture, soon after I received tenure, I was invited to participate in a conference focusing on issues of culture and state in Mexico. The conference participants included individuals who had conducted research about various regional Mexican revolutionary movements. Together, we fashioned a scholarly community, one that hoped to understand the relationship between a revolution made by ordinary people attempting to fashion a more just country, and the authoritarian postrevolutionary government that emerged. In our efforts to assess the relationships between such revolutionary processes and counterrevolutionary outcomes, we developed a perspective linking Foucault's ideas about power with those of Gramsci regarding culture. Crucially, we believed the peasants about whom we conducted research had partially altered not only postrevolutionary Mexico, but also the scholarly conversation about peasant and state.

The approach we developed has had the notable advantage of linking Mexican's daily political and personal habits to the construction of Mexico's postrevolutionary local, regional, and national governments. Indeed, we showed ways the instability of these institutions was linked to people's changing engagements with them.[17] Meeting at an international conference to share our ideas about what came to be known as "everyday forms of state formation," we presented the various essays that later emerged in *Everyday Forms of State Formation: Revolution and the Negotiation of Rule in Modern Mexico.*

The conference provided me with an opportunity to share aspects of my ethnohistorical research, including my emerging perception about the workings of culture. Indeed, building on the relationships between my empirical research and my research into an extensive array of works focusing on rural culture, I came to understand and define culture as "a people's evolving interpretation of the world and the ways that interpretation shapes the contours of daily life."[18] It was work that enabled me to consider some of the ways in which the dancers participated in the construction of Mexico's hegemonic, postrevolutionary government.[19]

If now, many years later, it is clear that our approach provided an original fashion through which to understand the politicization of Mexican peasants and the Mexican postrevolutionary state, what enthralled me at the time about the work was the opportunity to see and communicate the fashions in which impoverished male but particularly female forms of behavior played not only personal but also political roles in the development of postrevolutionary Mexico. Thus, in my article "Torching La Purísima, Dancing at the Altar," a northwestern Michoacán world emerges as more than simply the arena where rival male-dominated church and state vied for control. Rather, through focusing on the thinking and the behavior of rural women who at times worked together, at times competed with one another, and at times used elements of either government or church to benefit themselves, women's worlds—as power-laden as they were intimate—emerge from the historiographic shadows. So too did the fact that it was the tasks women were compelled to perform that allowed an agrarian capitalist structure to persist.[20]

While approaches to modern Mexican history were changing, so too were approaches to historical writing. I was fortunate enough to be invited to take part in the development of an original approach to historical representation called "innovative historical writing."[21] In part, such writing is based on conventional history's great advantages—its commitment to explain change over time, its abilities to re-create historical actors with specificity, and thus, as behavior differs from person to person, from space to space, from moment to moment, to remember and render the richly contingent examples of human behavior through time. Still, the new theoretical and at times literary approach challenged the fashions in which, since the nineteenth century, many historians have ignored prevalent artistic and scientific innovations,[22] instead maintaining a form of composition in which an omniscient Godlike narrator uses a linear approach to time through which he or she organizes and communicates conclusions about individuals' historical experiences.[23]

Participating in this innovative theoretical and linguistic opening inspired me to create a bolder, more expansive perspective on Latin American gendered history, one that struck me as consistent with Latin America's own extraordinary cultural complexity. Thus, individually, I wrote six of what became ten post-tenure articles, each of which attempted to reveal as vividly as possible the shapes, the colors, and the meanings of previously invisible or misunderstood female worlds. Perhaps because of the complex reproduction of various temporal movements, the development of multiple voices and perspectives, the re-creation of these sensual worlds replete with color, sound, scent—these articles at times have been likened to nearly cinematic reckonings of worlds that previously were ignored.

In retrospect, too, the intellectual risks of my approaches emerge. After all, academics trained as historians of the US South and of Latin America were not encouraged to consider or initiate ways that literary or musical or psychological or visual forms of representation could be linked to those of history. Yet the longstanding erasure of crucial elements of Mexican female experience, the urgency to communicate the situations of many of the individuals whose histories emerged from my research, suggested that my training and experience could be used to more clearly and elegantly display the complex historical activities of the people about whom I wrote.

In my articles, I thus built interrelated historical nests of female activity, thought, and feeling, all communicated through a linguistic style drawing on Mexican women's temporal, gestural, sensual, and linguistic experiences through time. These are worlds redolent with color, light, hue, fragrance, but also plight, as throughout the periods I analyzed, women lacked equality before the law. Moreover, each of these essays—while connected to one another and to the larger emerging field of Mexican cultural history—displayed complex microhistories based on extensive original research into the gendered histories of the Americas, religious belief and practice, and comparative approaches to temporality.

While the first of these articles, "Torching La Purísima, Dancing at the Altar," places the Ario dance within the larger framework of the responses to *Cardenismo*, it particularly ponders issues that earlier went unquestioned. That is, it wonders about the supposedly eternal and deep relationship between women and the church, about La Purísima in relationship to female parishioners, and even about an assumed female uniformity of behavior and of purpose. By developing a post-structural approach to the essay's attention to women's responses to church and state, I was able to illuminate the ways women's choices within that postrevolutionary context proved to be exceptionally vivid, demanding, at once difficult and attractive.[24]

"When I Was a Child, I Danced as a Child, but Now that I am Old, I think About Salvation: Concepción González and a past that would not stay put"[25] is an article in which I problematize conventional historians' dependence on linear narrative strategies, strategies in which linear organizations of time are linked to the unstated assumption that with each passing moment, people experience greater happiness, equity; deeper experiences of what often has been understood as progress itself. In fact, the Ario historical characters' varied responses to the Mexican revolution's abilities to improve or undermine their circumstances encouraged me to complicate the narrative by placing the characters within the temporal contexts they themselves preferred.

At the same time, by drawing on the array of Catholic priests I interviewed and on the previously unknown historical documents I discovered, I created a fictionalized priest. As he revealed his thought patterns in the article, he emerged as a person ruminating on women's extensive materialism, their troubles behaving with the modesty God expected. That is, the historical behavior I fictionalized revealed him as an individual truly persuaded that the revolution had undermined women's chances for eternal life, a priest alert to the women's perspectives with which he disagreed.

Within the context of the democratic and empathic temporal structure of the article, an approach allowing historical characters to weigh in on the significance of their behavior, unpredictable consequences emerged. In particular, a woman known for dancing in the Ario church, and in fact the only surviving dancer located in Ario, expressed no pride in her youthful revolutionary behavior. Communicating no desire to take credit for her adventurousness or for her courage, she instead seemed to hope that her past could go unnoticed. Thus, I found myself compelled to create a world reflecting not simply my personal enthusiasm about the dance, but also the modesty and timidity she expressed about its recollection.

In "As Though They Meant Her No Harm, María Enríquez Remade the Friends Who Abandoned Her—Their Intentions, Their Possibilities, Their Worlds—Inviting Them (Perhaps, It Is True) to Dance,"[26] I hoped to alert readers to the then ramshackle world of Mexican documentation, the ways an archival "organizational" scheme informed by theft, hoarding, political destruction of documents, censorship, and—in the case of some men and most women—centuries of illiteracy made my discovery of the scattered documentation about María Enríquez's sexual-assault trial remarkable.[27] Further, in the article I also continue to consider some of the ways historians' conventional linear approaches have normalized men's physical and emotional experiences (including those of warfare and diplomacy), while simultaneously ignoring the array of female experiences in northwestern Michoacán.

Analyzing the contrast between impoverished male and female temporal experiences in their daily lives in northwestern Michoacán, I demonstrate that there, most men worked the fields from before early light until past sundown.[28] Their temporal experiences could thus be charted in linear ways. The women, however, found themselves forced into constant and ever-changing work routines. No break at dusk for them; rather, the women experienced multiple, enduring demands for their labor. Indeed, I called impoverished Michoacán women's temporal experiences "ghost time," to suggest the persistent and persistently unseen and unappreciated character of women's work routines.[29]

But women not only bore temporal burdens that men did not. Women also suffered sexual assault.[30] In Enríquez's court case, she pointed out that she was both sexually assaulted by Antonio Mendoza and abandoned by friends, neighbors, and relatives. Further, as I point out, she was a woman alert to the social and historical reasons for which she was abandoned. Developing her own historically empathic approach to her trial testimony against her alleged assailant, Antonio Mendoza, I assessed the depth of generosity that characterized Enríquez's responses to those who refused her assistance.

Thus, her friend, Antonio Mendoza's sister, failed to help her because, I suggest, the sister would have learned through familial experiences similar to those of Enríquez herself, how little females were valued in Michoacán.

As for her own sister, Enríquez attributes her refusal to help to an understandable youthful ignorance. And indeed, Enríquez even went so far as to maintain that the wealthy women walking past her on the way to church must have ignored her request for help because of an easily understood mistake. Certainly, they saw Enríquez not as an assault victim nor even as a young, female stranger seeking help. Rather, they must have mistaken her as a woman whom, as Enríquez implied, was culturally acceptable for all to degrade—Pachita la loca, (Pachita, the Crazy Woman).

Returning to scholarly conversations about the historical positions of women throughout the Americas, I wrote for *History and Theory* an innovative article entitled "Talking Back to Frida: Houses of Emotional Mestizaje," coupled with the meta-narrative, "Talking Back to 'Talking Back to Frida: A Meta-Reflection,'" which discusses the perspective informing "Talking Back to Frida."[31] In fact, in "Talking Back to Frida," the physical world, people's relationships to that world, their connections to houses, flowers, plants, and physical possessions, including furniture and costumes, all emerge almost as characters that communicate elements of individuals' experiences through time. That is, those specific natural and physical possessions are so keenly understood in their relationships to their owners that the objects come close to possessing lives of their own.

Linking historical, fictional, and poetic approaches, the essays place the Mexican artist Frida Kahlo at a meal with a fictionalized version of my German-Jewish grandfather and his fellow lawyer friends. Within this domestic arena, the fictionalized Black servant who cooked and served the meals emerges as Kahlo's and the readers' guide both to the exquisite home and, most especially, to the servant's highly insightful assessments of her white employers, living and dead.

As Kahlo moved through some of the times and spaces I remembered and about which I had conducted oral history interviews,[32] she depended on her outsider's gaze to consider key historical elements of deep southern racism, classism, sexism, and anti-Semitism; by doing so, Kahlo was able to assess some elements of a deep southern society and culture filled with acts of injustice and of generosity, the very culture that disturbed and then motivated me as a young scholar. Then, as the essay moves into Kahlo's own physical and psychological environments, into the Mexican rooms in which she lived, I reconsider her experiences by coding color to emotion, brushstrokes to her actual historical experiences with left-wing politics, with Leon Trotsky, with her beloved and abusive husband Diego Rivera, all suggesting elements of her complex artistry and something of the ways her pain and narcissism defined her artistic and political approaches to the Mexican poor.[33]

María Enríquez receives the last word here, comparing and contrasting her economic and physical experiences with Kahlo's and with my own. In her discussion, Enríquez reveals elements of her thoughtful personality, her awareness that those who deserted her were more than neighbors, relatives, and friends capable of abandoning her, but also, at times, "on good days, in good light,"[34] people who proved to be more generous than they had been on the day they abandoned her. And here again, Enríquez reveals deep empathy and also expansive understandings of what could emerge as a United States and a Mexico informed by more equitable social relations.[35]

Without completely recognizing it at the time, in *Setting the Virgin on Fire* and my subsequent articles, I used language itself as a means to display not simply the advantages and burdens a male-dominated language had granted to men, but also as an opportunity to develop an original, particularly literary rendition of Mexico's history informed by gender-, class-, and age-based divisions. At the same time, I continued to seek a scholarly approach open to individuals' inner worlds, an approach sadly absent from many historical studies.[36]

When the opportunity to take part in a longstanding Los Angeles poetry community emerged, I jumped at the chance to participate and thus began a process of poetic training, which itself would expand into formal poetic training in a multiyear master class taught by David St. John. This study and practice led to my three published poetry collections, *Body Bach, Piano Glass/Glass Piano*, and *The Macon Sex School: Songs of Tenderness and Resistance*, each of which sought to enter the historical imaginations of multiple characters, and each of which in many ways depend on my longstanding musical training and Latin American and Deep Southern historical and ethnohistorical research. Each of these collections of poems—indeed, each poem itself—drew on what I'd learned from my international research, using facts, observations, thoughts, and experiences to inform the imaginative work involved in writing poems.[37]

Each of these collections is alert to poetry's concerns with the connections between interior and exterior life, poetry's musical and physical origins, its embrace of gesture to develop gendered worlds of sensual and intellectual experience. Crucially, all of my poetry collections, like all of my history books and articles, are alert to the repeated misogynist and life-threatening dangers of international and domestic fascism, the ways those fascisms attack gendered psyches, sensibilities, and bodies. Both *Body Bach* and *Piano Glass/ Glass Piano* can be read as poetic histories; *Body Bach* is a poetic history of sensualized temporal events experienced by an array of Deep Southern, Spanish, and Latin American men and women. Through the development of images of water, gemstones, clothing, and dance, this historical mediation invites readers into subconscious realms of experience. Even more character driven, *Piano Glass/Glass Piano* is based on its female narrator, who found herself compelled to use the depth of her powers to transform entrapped and abused women and men.

The Macon Sex School: Songs of Tenderness and Resistance is a series of poetic songs and psalms in which an array of women uses their voices and their bodies to challenge centuries of authoritarian gendered decisions. Confronting long-held assumptions that females matter little compared to males, each woman merges intellect, body, and voice to portray concrete and empathic fashions to undermine centuries of racialized, religious, and gender-based prejudices and essentialisms and to re-create affective worlds.

Viewed distinctly, these intellectual pathways into social, cultural, gendered history—toward the tonalities—the orchestration of poetry might initially appear to be unrelated. After all, historians' principle concerns remain the discovery of human behavior contextualized in order to explain either stasis or change over time. Poets, while at times locating their poems historically, possess no such relationship with nor responsibility toward time. Poetry, initially a form of communication linking language, music, and dance,[38] remains a form enabling poets to draw on the very emotional realms that historians, entrapped by limited documentation, often have found themselves unable to consider.

This sort of limitation frequently felt daunting. Worlds, experiences of those worlds I knew existed, had not been set down in language. Nonetheless, those experiences, and most particularly those experiences that various Latin Americans offered me, and even more specifically the complex historical array of experiences the dancers granted to me, have informed my efforts to expand on Latin American cultural and gender studies and to accept the gifts provided by literary studies. When I was invited to write a book blending my more strictly historical perspectives with the historical innovations I developed, I suddenly decided to create a bridge between what I view as Paz's unconscious bias toward gender informing his gendered approach to time, and the dancers' complex, courageous, and original approaches to the temporal.

Although the dancers lived and embodied much about the worlds Paz poetically imagined, his failure ever to meet them, either imaginatively or in life, calls for a specifically open approach, one alert both to Paz's gifts and inadequacies regarding gender, and one particularly alert to the complicated forms of communication the women demonstrated.[39] Indeed, the power of coupling a scholarship involved with specific individuals who, during Mexico's postrevolutionary era, transformed women's temporal possibilities with the startling approach to temporality that Paz devised can prompt a highly different way of seeing, feeling, dancing the world. It can also generate a new approach to the dancers, to Paz, one that can emerge as a distinct form of dance.

In *Dancing on the Sun Stone: An Exploration of Mexican Women and the Gendered Politics of Octavio Paz*, then, the formal distinctions between history and poetry become ways to develop connections between the dancers and Paz. Indeed, precisely because the dancers and Paz (read: historians and poets) communicate differently, it seems important to draw on both modes of communication to enable the women and Paz, ever more deeply, to dance both separately and together, in time, in space, through my specific assessments of them. Thus, this study will draw together historians' concerns with contingency, context, and specificity with poets' sensitivities to musical, physical, and emotive lives.

Dancing on the Sun Stone, then, seeks to create a language through which the Michoacán dancers and their critics, who entrusted me with key elements of their worlds, the Paz of *Sun Stone* and his critical studies can speak to one another through me. In doing so, readers can consider the changing meanings of time, sensuality, gender, and revolution. Indeed, this temporal conversation between the dancers and Paz emerges as a complex, multifaceted bridge taking them, you, and me into a Mexican world alert to some of the ways Paz remained unaware of the vastness and complexity of female temporal experience, and also to the fashions that the embodied language the women created, the specific fashions in which the women danced on the sun stone, altered Mexican historical possibilities themselves.

CHAPTER ONE

Walking Into History

When Women Made Tortillas,
Danced, and Reconfigured Time

In 1937, Michoacán women seized a church, and by dancing there, they altered time, space, historical possibilities, and themselves. What, though, led them there? How were females raised and compelled to experience temporality in ways deeply unlike male experiences of time?[1] How had girls and women raised in a culture demanding female modesty, chastity, near invisibility from crucial public events, altered their lives? How did that alteration enable the revolution, as it made its way to Michoacán, to itself clamor for a more inclusive response to the women there?

And how did I learn about them? Considering that I was both invited by prominent scholars to study the region and also warned against studying Michoacán, what about the place itself lured me there? Further, what about Michoacán—particularly a mestizo Michoacán that emerged on the backs of, and close to, what remained of its Tarascan Indigenous world—began to share crucial aspects of its histories with me?[2] How did I discover, even come to define, its cultures? What about those cultures depended on women and girls? And what about the vast feminine realms informed the Michoacán political culture that the revolutionaries sought to re-create? Indeed, how did the women there use their bodies to reshape the revolution?

I entered Michoacán in a particularly physical way. Previously, it was a world I knew only through the secondary literature I'd read and most especially through the primary documentation about it that I discovered in Mexico City archives. That is, even before discovering the level of subconscious bias against women and the deep ambivalence regarding female bodies, I developed a grassroots physical approach to what was, initially, a new world to me. In order to know the worlds about which I was to write—if clearly a partially latter-day version of them—I began walking them.

I walked to understand the sort of ground on which Michoacanos had walked, worked, made love, and raised children.[3] I walked to learn, as deeply as I could, what sort of territory had so entranced the sixteenth-century Spaniards; had prompted war after war over land, over religion. I walked to take in, as walkers can, a sense of this area that remained deeply rural, this area where farmers continued to grow the wheat and corn that made it part of Mexico's breadbasket. In particular, I walked in order to create a connection to places that certainly were not my own in any ethnic fashion, connections I hoped might encourage Michoacanos to share their histories with me.[4]

As a scholar and writer focusing on gender and ethnicity fortunate enough to have conducted extensive research and written in many forms about female historical experience, I have come to recognize that Mexico and its history existed only because of female participation in that history. Nonetheless, particularly during my initial explorations in Ario, in Zamora, in Morelia, in the Tarascan village of Jarácuaro, in the former Tarascan capital of Pátzcuaro—I encountered only men. There they were, everywhere in charge of archives, of banks, in the agrarian reform headquarters. The women I initially discovered tended to be servants. The Tarascan women sweeping the ground in the Zamora plaza with such Sunday morning vigor. The servant—also a Tarascan—hired by a well-off mestiza woman to turn small orbs of painted clay into pearls adorning quinceañera dresses.[5] The hotel employees who laundered my clothing.

In short, I began wondering about the social structure,[6] about where the other women were, where they had been, what their experiences before and during the Cardenista revolutionary era had been. In the event, these questions enabled me to understand something about the barriers to female civil and religious equality there. What might it have been to be trained to emulate La Purísima, the regional patron saint and certainly the Virgin Mary in her most modest and reticent guise? What was it like for the girls and women, most of whom lived lives depending on men who frequently worked as poorly paid day laborers on nearby ranches or estates? In particular, how did women experience time in a place characterized by both an extraordinary need for women, and a subconscious bias against that need and against the complex ways women lived?

While my questions about gender, race, and class prompted my initial inquiries into the experiences most people lived before and during the Cardenista period, it was only after my years conducting research in Michoacán that women's and men's crucial *relationships* with time itself came to seem so urgent to me. After all, in a place where women were encouraged to behave in exceptionally modest fashions while simultaneously undertaking persistent workloads, I had determined that the sort of unappreciated time women experienced deserved the name "ghost time."[7] In particular, as I hope to show here, women not only experienced the sort of finite, linear, birth-to-death temporality all people do. In addition, these Michoacán women—in part because of their gender—developed specific experiences occurring in time, experiences unlike those of men because of female relationships with time, relationships leading some of the Michoacán women to dance.[8]

To consider (and in some regard, to reconsider) that temporal background leading to the dance, it is useful to pay attention to the day-to-day female time-scape, a time-scape that for most women was filled with a particularly extensive type of housework, itself a sort of work depending on female physical engagements with time. As important as it is to enter those worlds, it is also crucial to ponder how women performed their tasks, and how these performances affected women—how, I suggest, those tasks emerged as full-bodied tasks that emerged as a sort of dance practice.

To see women and men's prerevolutionary and revolutionary experiences through a gendered lens is to discover women compelled to use their bodies in time to perform multiple, uncelebrated tasks men could not or would not undertake. Yet it is also to see that while many men, including revolutionary men, paid limited attention to female time use, all sorts of women themselves did. It would in fact be women's changing engagement with time that defined their dance in the church, the dance revealing what a women's revolutionary movement could be.

When Populating a Territory, Feeding and Tending its People Emerged as Female Destiny

The irony of the largely unnoted world of female time use is that in northwestern Michoacán, as elsewhere, it was women who used their bodies in time to populate the region. In fact, female temporal involvement with courtship, childbearing, and child-rearing somehow suggested that it would be females, and never males, who also were charged with using their bodies in time to perform other unpaid tasks related to sustaining and enhancing life.

How, then, did females and males experience this world of gendered temporality? Women's experiences in populating northwestern Michoacán depended on their capacities to transform matter into flesh that would fill otherwise unpopulated worlds. Yet the concrete details describing courtship and sexual experiences there have, likely for reasons emerging from a culture depending on female sexual "purity," largely remained hidden. Indeed, in northwestern Michoacán girls and boys, men and women, encountered one another within a world steeped with efforts to maintain a segregation separating people by ethnicity and class.[9] As Ario native Rafael Ochoa pointed out, in early childhood, boys and girls began to recognize that the poor and the wealthy were not to socialize. Certainly, by the time they grew older, impoverished men came to believe that "wealthy women wanted things we poor men could not provide."[10]

Still, within this socially divided world, through experiences likely marked by happiness and need, women and men began courting one another, sharing time, and developing connections ultimately dependent on women using their bodies and psyches to re-create the world. That is, through their pregnancies, women populated villages, towns, the country itself, filling the territories with new people.[11] Further, it is worth remembering that Michoacán women did this at a time and in a place lacking electricity and running water, a place without modern medical practices. Thus, women risked their lives with each pregnancy and birth. And at a time and place where pregnancy itself was assumed to be beneficial and practice of non–Church-sanctioned birth control was understood as sinful, women became pregnant frequently.[12]

The temporal and physical implications for women were crucial. After all, depending on the perspective, pregnancy enabled or compelled a woman to experience her own body as it changed through the duration of the pregnancy. Pregnancy enabled or compelled the woman to experience aspects of the temporal growth within. At the point of birth, the woman experienced time as an instance during which she used her body to relinquish new life into a world her own temporal experiences of pregnancy had altered. Then, once her child or children were born, the woman drew on her feelings and perspectives in time to feed the baby, to tend to the child's early physical and emotional needs before the child could speak, crawl, or walk. Through this series of uniquely female engagements with time and matter, women enabled children to themselves experience two distinct temporal and spatial realms.

How, then, were many northwestern Michoacán women compelled to use time after the birth of their babies? Certainly, Octavio Paz's description of Mexico as a place defined by brutal temporal regimes demanding violent death to allow the world to persist, combined with his frequent ignorance about women's temporal experiences themselves, remains striking. At the same time, it is true that many men, including those who seemingly revered women, themselves undermined the significance of women's time use.[13] For example, Michoacán native and schoolteacher José Corona Nuñez assuredly praised his mother for attending primary school in Morelia, "for learning to play the piano and sing and above all, learning to ride a horse," while also insisting that she was "a housewife, nothing more, sweeping and cleaning."[14] And Ario native Luis Amezcua insisted that "women do no work here."[15]

Within this cultural arena in which the necessity of women's overwork often went unnoted, even unseen, Ario native Concha Méndez illuminated key aspects of women's use of time. A member of a prominent Ario family and a religiously devout individual, Méndez said she had spent time visiting "many impoverished women."[16] It may have been on these visits when Méndez observed that the consistent, demanding tasks assigned to women, and especially to those assigned to the impoverished female majority, amounted to what she called "women's destiny."[17] To her, that female destiny was defined by the cultural demand that women fill their time with "*cocinando, lavando, planchando*"; that is, cooking, washing, and ironing clothing.[18]

It was that remark that prompted me to think about how women used time to perform those tasks. At that time in Mexico, it was almost always women, rather than men, who cooked. A longstanding historical decision that only females were to engage time and matter in this fashion, it was also a decision that defined much about female time use.[19] Because of large families, women often found themselves spending as many as three daily women-hours making tortillas.

To enter the worlds in which women fed people and, indeed, to observe the ways women used time in this transformative fashion, it is worth imagining a woman rising during the dark, predawn hours. Depending on gestures she taught herself, she would have moved away from her mate amid the emerging sounds of birdsong, cows lowing, the murmur of her own thoughts. Then, moving toward embers of the previous day's fire, she quickly worked the flames into the smallest possible blaze, due to the price of wood. Walking a few steps toward the ears of corn, the lime, the cooking pot, she placed the ingredients in the pot, waiting for the lime juice to season the corn as the kernels softened.

Bending into a crouch, the woman began grinding the corn into a sort of flour. Then, depending on her ideas about the shape and look of tortillas, she used her arms, hands, fingers to arrange and flatten rounds. Placing them on the griddle, holding the griddle over the fire, she waited a moment, flipped the tortilla-to-be, waited another moment, then removed the tortilla from the fire to place it in a basket. Then she repeated this array of gestures, as tortillas were the dietary staple for her growing family.[20]

Along with tortillas, women also used their bodies in time and space to prepare a multi-scented, multihued array of other foods, including, in many homes, beans and squash. And in the homes of the wealthy where—again—only women cooked, many women employed as servants organized schedules to enable them to prepare a vast and complex array of dishes, including chicken, beef, tamales, and hot chocolate.[21]

As for the female "destiny" of "lavando y planchando" (i.e., the tasks of tending clothing), northwestern Michoacán women participated in the multifaceted female journeys that caring for clothing entailed in a culture where appearance deeply mattered.[22] Again, these tasks assigned to females depended on female abilities to transform matter in time. To return to the post-tortilla-making homes is to watch the women moving through the homes, determining which family members' clothing needed to be cleaned. Collecting the clothes, the women made bundles of the soiled clothing.[23]

Walking outdoors, the women would meet with neighboring women also carrying bundles of soiled clothing. Then, together, the women began their walks through the villages' gorgeous and ever-changing physical backdrops.

On these to-the-stream walks, women created and experienced connections not simply with the invisible landscapes time provided for women to color with their activities, but also with space. Although the territory they walked was territory over which an array of men had made war, contesting its ownership and its meanings, this territory also came to be marked by the women's to-the-stream walks, their to-the-church walks, their walks when men befriended or threatened them. Making temporal claims on this territory, the women also likely recognized that the territory was potentially dangerous, prompting protective attitudes toward one another.

Assuredly, these journeys through the villages on foot also enabled the women to use their time to gain awareness about the social and cultural contours of the area. Walking past the large and showy buildings surrounding the plaza, the women observed a communicative architecture. Buildings there revealed the social significance of outer displays of wealth and prominence. There were the homes of wealthy landowners, whose wherewithal provided additional rooms and the ability to hire women to make and provide more bountiful meals. There was the church itself, where parishioners were told of a belief system at once welcoming to all but also concerned to communicate demands regarding female modesty, chastity, silence, and the unstated commitment to female overwork.[24]

While it was women's overwork that granted the men opportunities to join together in *tertulias*, gatherings during which they shared gossip and drink, the women, too impoverished and too busy to relax over drinks, may well have made their walks into ambulatory tertulias. During these tertulias, the women likely created a sort of social alchemy, turning their knowledge about fellow villagers or strangers into useful, at times protective information.[25]

Women living during a time and in a space lacking protective social institutions may have talked with one another about how, earlier, the Zamora woman Maria Enriquez had taught herself a form of protection against her erstwhile boyfriend who physically assaulted her.[26] And when Ario villager Carmen Barragán walked to the stream to do laundry, she may have mentioned that even men, like her father, at times found themselves threatened by a boss who paid them inadequately. About how he and fellow workers plotted resistance on the landlord's own property, unbeknownst to him.[27] Other women might have shared what information they had regarding relatives who had immigrated to the US. Who cared for them? Did women there also provide food for their men?[28]

When the women arrived at the stream, they likely depended on an extensive and growing knowledge about their capacities to change the appearance of clothing. Using powers of observation, arms, and hands, they placed the soiled garments in the water. Depending on their strength, they pressed the garment against the rocks-become-washboards. And again. And another garment, as the women turned soiled clothing into clean. As the women-as-laundry-women worked, alert to each garment's situation—a rip here, a stain there—the women demonstrated something about both the demands of their "destinies" and the flexibilities they developed living out those obligations.

When Revolutionary Teachers Altered Gendered Time

While, assuredly, a widespread social revolution granting economic, political, and personal rights to all, and most especially to the women who had long lacked them, would have transformed Michoacán in crucial ways, such a revolution did not take place there. Instead, in northwestern Michoacán, few participated in the 1910 revolution. It was the 1926–1929 counterrevolution that prompted many Michoacán men to mount guerrilla war against other men as they fought over issues of belief and land. What, though, of the women there? In northwestern Michoacán women were trained to be more devout, more politically complacent, more silent than men. They were expected to perform their maternal and "predestined" tasks.

Still, because of Michoacanos' counterrevolutionary fervor, Lázaro Cárdenas, himself a Michoacano, mobilized Michoacanos—who proved mainly to be mestizo men and a few mestiza women—to develop a revolutionary program designed to divide up landed property, to train students to see the government rather than the church as a central protective institution, to train children in basic math, reading, and writing.

What, then, did this program and its initiatives have to do with gendered time? One way to consider this issue is to follow two Michoacán female teachers as they experienced time in ways men did not. That is, the Mexican revolution provided no female legal equality. It provided no official transformation of a gendered temporal universe in which females were expected to bear and raise children, to fill their house with tasks that sustained others. Still, within that constraining context, two female revolutionary teachers—Angelina Acosta and Evangelina Rodríguez Carbajal—each experienced revolutionary temporality in gendered ways. In both of their cases, experience alone outside the home remained perilous because of their gender. And yet, in each case, these women experimented with gendered temporality in a postrevolutionary setting.

Rodríguez Carbajal was a Protestant from Morelia and a school inspector, whose occupational obligations included assessing the work of other teachers to determine whether it complied with the revolutionary curriculum. To observe Rodríguez Carbajal riding a horse into northwestern Michoacán, where she would undertake her inspecting chores, is to see a woman who dressed in stylish ways finding herself in unfamiliar temporal territory.[29]

That is, as a Protestant in a deeply Catholic part of Michoacán, Rodríguez Carbajal found her students' temporal perspectives startling, even wrongheaded. As she inspected the students and their families, she encountered an unfamiliar temporal universe in which individuals made decisions according to a Catholic time clock. Theirs was a temporal world that included an array of holidays, feast days, and saints' days. To her, such slavish devotion to the Catholic perspective was difficult to understand. She found their tradition "antique" and believed their practice of their religion made them into "complete fanatics."[30] Certainly for her, such customs—she did not understand them as religious obligations or pleasures—stood in the way of proper revolutionary behavior, of the construction of a new, more progressive time-scape. An outspoken, even impassioned individual, she made her perspective about this misuse of time clear.

As for the female temporal destinies compelling women to bear and raise children, to perform an array of duties helping others to sustain life, she said nothing in her reports focusing on rural life. Why? Why would this woman known for her dramatic approaches to changing the world in time have ignored this crucial way many women found themselves using time? Perhaps the widespread cultural evasion of both female physical danger and the conventional use of women to grant their time to provide men with chances to avoid the levels of overwork women performed was so deeply ingrained that even a woman like Rodríguez Carbajal failed to notice.

Angelina Acosta, another Michoacán revolutionary woman, experienced gendered revolutionary time distinctly. A Zamora native, she was a youthful

Catholic spinster with considerable pedagogical training. As a female, she knew her performance of her job in the village of La Rinconada, outside of Zamora, proved perilous. As though recognizing the dangers women courted by appearing alone in the world, she invited her mother to accompany her to La Rinconada. And not only did Acosta's mother perform domestic tasks like cleaning and cooking, but also, as Acosta pointed out, her mother accompanied her from Zamora to La Rinconada "to protect me."[31]

In her classroom, Acosta developed an experiment with gendered revolutionary time. Understanding time as an opportunity to transform students' notions regarding reality, she was among the teachers in coeducational classes who invited both female and male students to participate in journeys of discovery and revelation. Within her classes, she tried to train students not only to understand the geographic range and reach of the country, its complex capacities to grow corn, avocado, and pimiento, but also to consider the country's physical bounty and human complexity.

Acosta, however, initially knew little about the challenges of rural life. From her hometown of Zamora, Michoacán's second city, she made her way to the nearby village of La Rinconada, hoping to make strangers into students and to enable them to think about themselves and the world in new ways. What proved striking about her approach, though, was her openness both to her own ignorance and to the fact that her students understood the rural world in ways she did not.[32] Thus, while at first she considered her students a bit "ignorant," she managed to make the material, however apparently abstract, at once concrete, useful, and inviting. Her lessons in literacy, math, and geography enabled her students to develop maps to unknown neighborhoods, forests. They trained the students to use numbers to count, tabulate, assess their possessions, their earnings, the scope of the governmental property being redistributed.[33]

Perhaps most importantly, Acosta came to view her position as more than an opportunity to share the information found in the handful of textbooks that made their way to Michoacán. She came to use class periods as opportunities to listen to her students, to begin to understand them, to see knowledge about them as itself reflective and crucial. Indeed, Acosta's classes became opportunities for her students to participate in co-creating their education.

How did these women experience, approach, and alter gendered time? How did they relate to a revolution that in many ways refrained from directly altering female participation in domestic labor? While each of them likely depended on other women to use time in conventional gendered ways, both Acosta and Rodríguez Carbajal forged new gendered temporal pathways. Certainly, in each of their cases, other female's domestic labor enabled them to experiment with gendered temporality. Nonetheless, though their personalities, creeds, and experiences differed, both women's experiences suggested that however hidebound prerevolutionary and even revolutionary gendered experiences had been for women and for men, however dependent revolutionaries remained on women's unpaid labor, the revolution's arrival in northwestern Michoacán granted some women and girls chances to experience gendered time in new ways.

To Politicize Time in the Women's Leagues

Neither Mexican revolutionaries nor counterrevolutionaries found female time use and overwork to be topics worthy of consideration. Instead, both local priests and local revolutionary land-reform leaders considered the revolutionary changes themselves, particularly the land reform and the revolutionary schooling, to be crucial. Priests went so far as to threaten men who accepted a plot of governmental land and parents who sent their children to the revolutionary schools with the perditions of excommunication.[34]

Within that context, few landless northwestern Michoacán men initially signed up to receive a plot of governmental land. To Zamora Cardenista agrarian leader Juan Gutiérrez, while it was the Catholic church that proved to be an institutional foe to the revolutionaries, within individual men's lives, it was the Catholic practice of their wives that kept the men from accepting land and supporting the revolutionary government. To persuade rural men to ally with the government and accept land, then, Gutiérrez turned to the wives and invited them to establish and participate in revolutionary women's leagues.[35]

By reaching out to the women, Gutiérrez styled himself as a rival suitor, a representative of a government seeking to claim the female time and attention they previously granted to the church. His invitation to women to develop women's leagues was an invitation to them to experience the world anew. Inviting them to develop new connections with one another in time and in space, he provided them with opportunities to experience time in new ways. That is, he granted them chances to attempt to alter their destinies.

Suddenly, each step from their homes to the meeting place for the revolutionary women's league became a step along a path, a roadway into a present and future each woman found herself forging. Unlike their "predestined" laundry walks they experienced after preparing and serving food to their families, unlike their journeys to celebrate mass, these walks to the women's league meeting existed in the sort of unique time-space that new ideas, new practices, and new and previously unnamed realities can present.

It is possible to see the meetings as instances during which the women presented themselves in novel fashion. Not so much in terms of wearing new clothing—few could have afforded to do so; rather, as the women there were of different ages and possessed differing views about religion, as northwestern Michoacán women had not previously gathered together in official discussions about local culture, the women likely used their body languages in new and distinct ways. The self-appointed leaders may have shown sprightly, even welcoming facial expressions as they spoke. The expressions of women possessing longstanding and extensive Catholic commitments may have been more serious, even grave.[36]

Together in a place with other women not to wash clothing, to assess village conditions, or to pray, the women were suddenly able to experience one another in novel fashions. The women perhaps realized they mattered then and there not only as mothers, as women mending, washing, and ironing clothing, as tortilla makers, but as women sharing sources of thought and ideas about government. Suddenly the women's ideas about the governmental land reform, about the church's opposition to it, were important.

What, though, did the women discuss at the meetings? The central topic that leaders like Matilde Anguiano and Maria Loreto Pacheco brought up was Catholicism and, most especially, the efforts of priests and devout neighbors to undermine efforts to revolutionize the area.[37] While much about Catholic practice was at that point illegal, Anguiano and Pacheco noticed numerous remnants of Catholic organization and worship. These women were among the regional league leaders who assessed Catholic efforts to revive or retain aspects of Catholic religious behavior. Frequently they expressed their concerns about this persistence or resurgence in letters to Gutiérrez, denouncing the appearance of furtive priests and those "who engaged in deviation and fanaticism."[38]

Assuredly, members of the league disagreed with one another about faith, as liga member Esperanza Rocha pointed out. To the liga leaders and perhaps to some participants, the trouble was the continuing intensity of Catholic practice. To Rocha, and perhaps also to others, the fact that liga leaders criticized Catholic ritual behavior—celebrating Mass, wearing religious regalia, baptizing children—proved distressing. At root, this disagreement was about a belief system that understood itself as a reflection of a male God who created the world, its workings, and proscribed ways people were to use time within that world as opposed to those who found such an approach to belief incorrect.

If women's emergence as political spokespeople proved to be novel, so too was the fact that in the leagues women focused both purposely and inadvertently on gendered time use. According to Rocha, the leaders condemned those members who used their time to celebrate the sacraments, to attend church, or to baptize their children. That is, they raised the issue about how women were to understand and experience time. Were they to continue to allow time to be filled with prayers, preparation of festive foodstuffs, acts of charity, and devotion? Or was time gendered in other, less regimental ways? Could time emerge as a territory upon which women freely created and expressed their ideas and sentiment?

Women in the revolutionary leagues shared neither age nor religious inclinations. They did not always agree with one another. And yet in the leagues Michoacán women experimented with new ways to connect to time, to appear in time, to consider time use, to behave as they had not before. While previously what they said to one another at home, near the stream, in church, had not been understood as particularly crucial or political in any way, the league meetings opened opportunities for women to see the importance of their thoughts, feelings, and ideas. In the meetings, the members enacted instances of women agreeing and disagreeing with one another within a realm of newfound gender associations.

When a Dance Reconfigured Time and Space

The tones many Michoacanos used in their discussion of the dance with me included cadences of shock and surprise about the women who proved audacious enough to enter the church and remake it into a den of sensuality.[39] And assuredly, during this period, Catholics used church buildings as places for parishioners to celebrate Mass, to deliver or hear sermons, to confess, and to pray. The idea that women would seize a church building for a festive dance can suggest a deep division between a church demanding female sexual and social reticence and those women who claimed the building, using it as a place to dance.

Then, too, this was a period characterized by contests over property ownership—ownership itself based on long periods of theft and during the long Porfirian dictatorship, the legalization of property seizures. Perhaps much about the series of events surrounding and defining the dance can and probably should be understood as yet another in a series of Mexican conflicts over property. After all, in order to create a dance floor from a church sanctified with an array of Catholic icons—the images of Jesus, Mary, the saints adorning the church—two groups of opposing men entered the church and removed the images.

While the dance certainly reflected and prompted disagreements about female behavior and about property, it also emerged, I maintain here, as a complex series of temporal experiences. Through taking part in the events surrounding the dance, through dancing, the women used their bodies to experience and to demonstrate elements of their relationships with time. By reentering the temporal and social territory surrounding the dance, then, key aspects of the women's relationships with time itself emerge.

What, then, of those two groups of men, people who themselves probably did not understand the complexity of female relationships with time—who engaged in crucial events surrounding the dance? After all, northwestern Michoacán boys, then men, learned that their relationships with time were to allow their attempts to dominate women and, at times, to own property. Building on those cultural assumptions, a group of wealthy men took the time to enter the church and remove the iconography.[40] After they left the building, images in tow, a group of revolutionary men followed suit, entering the church. Assessing the church, the revolutionary men encountered religious images the wealthy men had failed to notice. Seizing those images, the revolutionary men took them to their homes.[41]

After taking afternoon siestas, the revolutionary men invited their wives, daughters, and girlfriends to walk with them to the plaza. This walk, however, emerged as no routine stroll through the village that for Méndez "had been so peaceful."[42] Rather, once the group arrived at the plaza, they found wood, arranged it, and lit a fire. As the wood blazed, the men and women tossed icon after icon into the flames, altering the hue and quality of the light. It was as though the blazing Ario plaza suddenly hosted an anticlerical fiesta.[43]

Moving into the church, the men and women entered a building that could scarcely be considered a neutral arrangement of building materials. Rather, the Ario church long reflected the viewpoints of those who built it and those who used it. The building itself had hosted priests using time to communicate through a series of sermons and hymns the notion that male-dominated religious and secular hierarchies were permanent, and that parishioners were to model their behavior after a Virgin styled as a model of female chastity, humility, and reticence.[44]

Not that night. Within the church building, a local band the revolutionaries had hired played raucous contemporary music.[45] Then the revolutionary men turned to the women and invited them to dance. That is, the men offered the women a choice. The women's respective decisions—their respective agreements to dance with their men in the church—amounted to the women's agreements to use their bodies in time differently. Those agreements reveal a particular cultural fearlessness about new experience and an ability to alter temporal custom.

That is, when the men invited the girls and women to dance, they invited people whose array of previous movements in time had allowed them to confound any temporal duality, any idea that the life of a girl or a woman could be defined in only linear or only circular terms. Some of these women, moving with time that night, bearing it, containing it, already knew much about its birth-to-death dimensions, their singular female participation in ushering in life, their unique involvement in nourishing that life, the necessity to join with one another to protect their own lives and those of others. By using their bodies that night to reveal and conceal their temporal expertise, they used their bodies in time as none had before.

To watch them is to watch them as they move against a church floor previously used as one of the accoutrements celebrating the landowners, the wealthy, the men. Trained to display consistent generosity toward others, the women did not diminish their partners' presences as they danced. Rather, dancing in time, possessing a vast compendium of temporal experience, the women suggested a distinct, more complex and abundant time use. Seizing on the permission they'd been granted, the women's dance at once maintained aspects of its genesis—their tortilla-making hours, their to-the-stream walks, their fervent interludes discussing protection, while demonstrating—there where La Purísima reigned, there in the church space where poor people had been ignored, there close to the alter where priests had clamored for female silence—an entirely original female rendition of time.

With each step, women hinted at the subversive possibilities that can emerge from the hidden, unappreciated destinies that had prompted their flexibilities. It was as though the societal demands for women to be everywhere working unseen no longer held. It was as though, too, the demands that women behave modestly and silently took place in a previous world. That night, women developed and demonstrated the flexibility to move time into and out of the linear, the circular, using their bodies there to suggest a recognition of church ritual and an embrace of sudden, newly defined liberties. That night in that church where demands for female silence and near invisibility had long persisted, the women used their bodies and minds to reclaim time itself, readjusting its dimensions in order to reconfigure gendered temporality.

CHAPTER TWO

From Killing Stone
to Gendered Time-Scape

Octavio Paz and the
Making of the "Sun Stone"

Because the Michoacán dancers revealed aspects of the extraordinary worlds they used their bodies to create, display, and alter, those women strike me as just the people to engage the Mexican master of imaginative temporality, Octavio Paz, in his remarkable 1957 poem "Sun Stone."[1] A poem in which a poet takes on a godlike role, "Sun Stone" emerges as a depiction of and an ode to time itself. It remains one poet's effort to reconstruct Mexican temporality, to reconfigure the human and the natural worlds.

In its 584 lines, it unfolds almost as an invitation into an alternative world in which Paz develops a male speaker who invites readers into the world within worlds Paz devised through his ruminations on Mexican time. And he is a speaker who, while finding that world highly sensual, profoundly natural, also finds it, initially, damaged.

To Paz, that damage reflects the Aztec use of the sun stone as a killing stone. Those sacrificial killings—necessary, the Aztecs believed, to keep the sun moving, to keep the world alive—emerged for Paz as a ruinous temporal pattern. To Paz, that pattern was repeatedly reproduced from the time of the Aztecs into the twentieth century. Thus, in my view, Paz made the poem an extensive rumination reflecting his specific yearning for what he saw as Mexican democracy.

Indeed, as though to suggest that Mexican time itself entrapped the population, Paz developed the circular structure of "Sun Stone." Certainly, it is a structure unusually alert to the importance of precontact Indigenous Mexico. Certainly, too, elements of Paz's approaches to Aztec society revealed elements of a humanizing sensitivity. Further, Paz's development of a circular literary structure itself contains and restrains particular aspects of temporal life, communicating Paz's views on Mexican governmental hierarchy. At the same time, by focusing only on male temporality, Paz's speaker failed to see the ways Mexican female behavior in time enabled Mexican history itself to unfold. Thus, an important concern for a chapter hoping to allow readers to focus on key elements of the poem from a gendered, democratic perspective emerges. What sort of literary approach might honor Paz's accomplishment while demonstrating its limitation?

Seeking to communicate an approach alert to its liberating hopes and limitations, I have developed a somewhat unusual strategy. A conversational approach, it is one that at times interrupts the flow of the prose to discuss elements of my responses to "Sun Stone." It depends on questions to readers, on visual and metaphoric explorations of Paz's approach, on ruminations on the fashion in which he devised an exploration focusing on Mexican power relations—relations he understood as nearly, but not completely, permanent. It is a strategy flexible enough, I hope, to lead readers into my own reading of Paz's "Sun Stone," a reading alert both to Paz's democratizing hopes and, because of the ways he emerged as tone-deaf to women's experiences, to its inadequacies. It is a strategy that, I hope, will reveal the fashions that Paz's "Sun Stone" emerged both as a clamor for a more open Mexico and as a gendered time-scape, a temporal universe relatively replete with opportunities for men, yet one utterly dependent on combinations of female invisibility and presence.

Precisely because "Sun Stone" can be read as a poem at once lamenting Mexico's temporal past and at the same time a plea for a more open, democratic future, a historical reading, one sensitive to the complexity of the population Paz purports to discuss, seems crucial. Yet precisely because many historians go untrained in poetics, just as few poets emerge as trained historians, it also seems important to employ this conversational strategy that reveals my questions about the poem, about Mexican history, even about the strategy itself. It is an approach dependent on questions to readers, to interruptions, to visual and metaphoric exploration of Paz's approach, all in the interest of suggesting the inner workings of Paz's poetics and of historical inquiry. Most especially, the chapter invites readers to consider the ways Paz's masterful "Sun Stone" depended on a disturbingly inequitable gendered time-scape, one in which female time use went ignored or misunderstood.

To Claim, To Reconfigure the Aztec Sun Stone

For "Sun Stone," Paz developed a poetic structure communicating his sense of the power of the ancient Aztecs' understanding of time's movements.[2] The poem frequently suggests that Aztec temporality proved corrosive—if ultimately impermanent. Central to Paz's rendition is a male speaker he developed and uses to lure readers into this poetic realm. A speaker portrayed through an array of poetic strategies—the evocation of nature, the understanding of dream territory as temporal territory, the re-creation of a sensualized world as a persona—the speaker is established early as the guide with whom readers are to identify, as the guide evoking the damaged world Paz depicts.[3]

The speaker emerges in a temporal world redolent with exquisite yet disturbing images. Initially, there is a seemingly unmediated innocence here, to the "tree deep-rooted yet dancing still."[4] Further, it is a tree that dances within and upon a circular framework revealed through "a course of a river that . . . comes full circle."[5] That initial innocence itself, though, is questioned when the speaker invites us into a future characterized as "the wilderness of days to come."[6] Suddenly, Paz's speaker discovers that those days-to-be possess "misery like a bird / whose song can turn a forest to stone."[7] That forest, one transformed through birdsong to stone, amounts to a declaration of some of the ways Paz understood Mexican temporality as itself an agent of death, capable of destroying humanity. Indeed, there the stone undermines "the imminent joys on branches that vanish."[8]

As though human behavior and the world itself were confined to experiences of darkness or light,[9] Paz's speaker moves from his recognition of the precarious killing stone in order to approach a woman. She emerges as an individual portrayed at once as a woman living through time and as temporality itself inhabiting a woman's body. Further, Paz's speaker characterizes that female body as a sun goddess, a female deity whose "body of light" is "filtered through an agate," whose gestures are "the color of a brisk and leaping day."[10] It is time possessing a body, time depicted *as* a female body.

By addressing that female body in time, Paz approaches her less as a conversational partner as he refrains from animating her, and more—it strikes me—as a listener, an individual made alert to his concerns about time. Expanding that gendered position, Paz's speaker maintains it is her body that demonstrates what time is, that time itself can be seen within her physicality "visible through your body."[11]

That is, by using the woman's body as a mirror of the world, he portrays her both as a mirror reflecting the world *and* as a reflection of Mexican history itself. As a reminder, in a memento mori of the site of the killing stone he depicts her belly as "a plaza full of sun."[12] He further maintains that her breasts are "two churches."[13] He even dresses her in corn, revealing his view of women as creatures connected to Mexico's longstanding basic (and natural) foodstuff.[14]

Claiming for himself a right to observe the body of the woman and to assess it,[15] the speaker invites readers, too, to share in his observations. Consider, then, an imagery that moves from the speaker's emotive and physical excitement to entrapment. He dresses the woman "in the color of my desires"[16] and travels her eyes "like the sea."[17] Through images of her eyes, in which "tigers drink their dreams,"[18] he evokes danger, characterizing her as ferocious and violent.

While he is alert to, even anxious about, this ferocity, the speaker portrays it as inescapable. And yet there, notwithstanding the collection of emotions he has marshalled and evoked—those involving objectification, male tropes of lust, exploration, and objectification—he stumbles into a particularly Mexican danger that he personifies as that of a specific woman. He continues his gestural engagement with the woman, his practice of surveying her, telling her "I travel your body like a forest, like a mountain path, that ends in a cliff."[19] That is, the speaker blithely dehumanizes the woman, telling her he moves "along the edge of your thoughts and my shadow falls from your white forehead."[20] Indeed, his shadow itself "shatters."[21]

There, as though grasping something about Mexican danger he has personified as that of a woman, he finds himself challenged, disordered. Something has occurred that has left him uncertain. Disoriented, the speaker finds that the journey along the edge of the woman's unexpressed thoughts proved deeply challenging, compelling him to persist "with no body."[22]

What, though, has happened? What does this encounter with Mexico as woman, with this woman as Mexico, hint about Paz's temporal and gendered perspective? Here it feels important to ponder Paz's gendered characterizations from a perspective sensitive to Mexican historical power relations. That is, through a language of movement, symbolism, and direct addresses to readers, Paz's speaker developed a woman as emblematic of longstanding preconquest violence. Thus, through a series of at times contradictory images, the woman emerges as here physically gorgeous, there all cruelty and denial. The male speaker receives the overt communicative power to contend with her, a power denied to the woman.

Although the woman and her thoughts were portrayed as able to push the speaker away, it was as though he found himself startled, bruised, yet able to continue. While the speaker now lacks a body, he continues to possess both a voice and the ability to move as he reminds the reader that he will persist, "groping my way."[23] The woman, though, has emerged as the Indigenous time-scape with which the speaker contends.

That is, instead of noticing the ways Mexico's historical temporalities depended on power relations granting females limited power, Paz silently re-invoked such relations. His is a Mexican temporality informed by his speaker's development of a female imbued with a curious blend of ability to deny elements of the male speaker's demands alongside an inability to emerge as an individual who herself traveled through and defined Mexican temporal realities. Thus, the woman has emerged as a version of a Mexican Indigenous time-scape with which the speaker engages not to celebrate female power or admiration of a specific woman, but rather only to reveal the challenges the speaker—in his, not her nor their—journey must confront.

Within a Postcolonial Temporal Labyrinth

Without a body, the speaker and his journey persist, as Paz allows him to continue his circular and descriptive journey, now moving from the woman depicted as an earlier Mexico into what appears to be a reflection of post-Indigenous, post-Spanish conquest Mexico, even postcolonial time.[24] Yet the speaker leads readers into and through a quite complex gendered temporality without poetic or temporal markers. This poem does not communicate a poetics alive to the actual events occurring once the Spaniards and their Tlax-calan allies defeated the Aztecs.[25] Thus, Mexico's caste system, its nineteenth-century liberal/conservative conflict, its independence wars, its implementation of dependent industrial capitalism, its 1910 revolution, its postrevolutionary reconstructions, and its female participation in and through those periods all go unmentioned.

Instead, while Paz continues to style his speaker as a sort of rambler, the speaker's purpose now becomes one of inner contemplation. It is as though he understands rumination on his thoughts, gestures, and experiences within the world, as a rumination that, if properly contemplated, could release him. His quest—his journey through the time-scape—is that of a man determined to understand. It is as though he views inner contemplation of himself, of his thoughts, gestures, and experiences within the world, as themselves elements that, if understood properly, could release him.

Yet, how? Probably because Paz understood Mexican temporality as repetitious and encasing, he ignored its workings. Thus, rather than allowing the speaker to specifically engage with the era's socioeconomic, political, religious, even spiritual life per se, Paz depicts the speaker as representing and engaging his emotional life, a male, emotive life readers are to understand as that of Mexico itself. Thus, the speaker proceeds as an individual now without a body, seeking a different Mexico. It appears that to Paz this was a quest for existential freedom, a sort of freedom he continues to depict as universal.

While previously Paz utilized the speaker's perspective of a woman to reveal his insights about Mexico, now, without a partner, without a body, fraught, the speaker begins to represent not the former Mexico the woman represented, but rather what Mexico could be. Thus, the speaker's gestures change as his journey does; his invitation to readers to continue to accompany him on that journey becomes a quest to encounter and experience existential freedom in a new Mexico.

In particular, within what has emerged as a confessional tapestry revealing the speaker's collection of insight and reaction to his personal experiences in time, he redefines time. Rather than treat time as an invisible element, as a backdrop for human experience, he personalizes it, granting time an emotive and interactive range and reach. It is—I believe—that grasp of time that prompts the speaker to initiate a quest for what emerges as another sort of relationship, another sort of time. The speaker himself confesses that he seeks not another woman, but rather "a single moment."[26]

What sort of moment, though? While previously Paz's speaker understood Mexico's array of moments as murderous, now he appears at times to view the moment's face as one of "storm,"[27] or "rain in a darkened garden."[28] He grants his moment the creaturely liveliness, like a bird.[29] Crucially, Paz makes the moment into something of an interactive mirror, one the poet uses as a personal historical looking glass. That is, it is a mirror into which his speaker peers at an array of girls and women siphoned from personal memories and historical reflections.[30]

Consider the speaker's reflection regarding procreation and childbirth. Suddenly peering into the mirror of his emotive life, he emerges able to generate daughters with no erotic nor physical relationships involved. Indeed, there is no courtship, however lush, inviting, or troubled. Rather, a series of daughters emerge, full-born, a seeming instant-made-flesh as the speaker finds himself able to create "grapes containing girls," who "spill out from the fruit."[31] The girls are born of the speaker's sudden whim.

Then, casting a wide net through history and mythology, the speaker encounters an array of women. Assuredly, he points out that he has forgotten their names; then, suddenly, he recalls them.[32] They include Melusina, a water nymph from French mythology; and Laura and Isabel, evoked by Petrarch and Garcilaso de la Vega.[33] There is Persephone, the queen of the Greek netherworld.[34] And there is María, Jesus's virginal mother.[35]

Notwithstanding the variety of characteristics of their lives and experiences, Paz erases distinctions among them. Rather, drawing them from memory, he makes them identical and repetitious symbols. Replete with identifying traits, devoid of them, in his hands they become "all the faces and none."[36] Creatures of time, creatures out of time, they become "all the hours and none."[37] Building on this oppositional approach, Paz's speaker initially identifies them as elements of a glorious natural world, filled with "all the birds."[38] Turning that on its head, he makes them into "ivy that creeps, envelops, uproots the soul."[39]

Why such memorable and forgettable names? And didn't the speaker portray women as weapons, as the embodiment of mortal danger, during the time of encounter with the Europeans? While initially puzzling, this portrayal of women from the time of the Aztecs into the postcolonial period enables the women to serve as reminders, even warnings of the persistence of the repetitious and continuing threats posed by "circular days that open out on the same patio, the same wall."[40] And not only are the places circumscribed by circular time, but the human opportunities the male speaker encounters are also limited. Indeed, the same places are populated by a single persona, as the journey makes "all of the names a single name, all the centuries a single moment."[41] For men, then, this encasing temporality proves threatening.

Within that realm, the speaker—now styled a more contemporary twentieth-century character—emerges as a man seeking female romantic partners. Reflecting on a series of trysts mirrored by the moment, Paz's speaker initially sees his personal past as one laden with opportunity. That is, the speaker in his relationships with the moment seems to understand time as responsive to his needs. As he put it, "this night is enough, . . . that never stops revealing to me where I was, who I was, what your name is, what my name is."[42] The bounty of that moment, of that night, prompts the speaker to reflect on an extensive affective life, one he locates at once within memory and within the Mexican geographic landscape.

For instance, he asks himself if he made summer plans with a woman named Phyllis, the woman he describes through "the two dimples in her cheek, where sparrows come to drink the light."[43] He further inquires about a woman named Carmen. Was it she on the Reforma who told him that "the air is so crisp here, it's always October"?[44] Then, turning to yet another woman, the speaker asks whether they bought gardenias "in Perote."[45]

While the romantic arena in which Paz placed his speaker went unquestioned and thus normalized, it was a historically specific structure of relationships between men and women—a structure dictating that a man seek out and encounter a woman, offer her attention, and then sleep with her. Within this male-dominated approach to romantic relationships, the cultural perspective that it was to be men rather than women who defined the negotiation of romance was assumed.

Still, Paz's tone suggests that the repetitious nature of these arrangements distresses him. To be sure, the women differ, yet it appears that time itself continues both to move repetitiously and to promote repetitious patterns of behavior. His reflection about this use of time, about these relationships that took place in time, emerges as a plaintive chant about "someone combing her hair, . . . rooms, places, streets, names, rooms."[46]

A complaint revealing that Mexico's repetitious time-scape amounted to a series of imprisoning circular pathways, it is a complaint reminding readers that those institutional and habitual pathways possessed personal consequences for Mexican men. That is, the speaker deplores a postcolonial temporality that, like the earlier Indigenous and postconquest periods, refused him different ways to engage time, to experience his life as a Mexican man.

As for the women—whether Phyllis, Carmen, the woman combing her hair, Persephone, Maria—they have emerged as a series of one-dimensional figures, at times motherly, at times flirtatious, at times violent. These renditions suggest ways that the speaker's journey has been no poetic exploration of ways Mexican gendered temporality depended on the very Mexicans—Mexican women—who found themselves disempowered by Mexican institutions. Rather, Paz has ignored Mexican women's far more extensive experiences of top-down governance, focusing instead on ways Mexican institutional life compromised men's capacities to emerge as fully human.

Thus, notwithstanding Paz's engagement with Indigenous temporality and his recognition that personal intimacy is power-laden, he has continued to portray women—those whose names he remembers and forgets, those who accompany him, those he blames for Mexico's inadequacies—as people he denies capacity to themselves engage this historico-poetic debate about Mexican women's and men's relationships with time.

Wartime Madrid, Redemptive Sex, and the Making of the Gendered Time-scape

Rather than locate the center of "Sun Stone" in Tenochtitlán, the Aztec capital that after the sixteenth-century Spanish conquest of Mexico emerged as the capital of colonial, then modern Mexico, Paz moves the speaker from the Mexico of the sun stone itself to Spain's capital, Madrid. Further, he places the speaker in the Spain of the 1936–1939 Spanish Civil War, a war widely understood as a dress rehearsal for World War II.[47]

Moving the poem spatially and temporally to a Madrid plaza during 1937, Paz sketches an array of events in a historico-poetic context through which, I argue, he reveals the key to the gendered time-scape he has politicized. There, in that 1937 Madrileña plaza, the speaker invites readers to observe a man and a woman. It is their behavior during a deadly firestorm of the war that arrests. As if to draw attention to the uniqueness of their behavior within that context, the speaker refrains from granting names to either the man or the woman.

Rather, I suspect, the couple are to serve as an alternative couple, their lovemaking behavior as an alternative approach to time. While the warriors and their superiors seized time and space, defining their function as a ground for murder, as houses that Paz characterized as bodies that were "brought to their knees in the dust"[48] amid "the hurricane drone of the engines," the couple uses their bodies to communicate a distinct human possibility, an alternative approach to and use of time and space. As Paz's speaker puts it, the couple "took off their clothes and made love to protect our share of all that's eternal."[49]

This nameless couple has suddenly emerged as purposeful, politicized. Paz implies that their lovemaking during this war was simultaneously a protest against their former lives and an enactment of another sort of life. Suddenly undermining conventional understandings about the workings of the world, the couple kissed "because two bodies naked and entwined, leap over time,... they return to the source."[50] In doing so, they erase individuality, time itself, emerging anew "in a single body, a single soul."[51]

A couple stripping to make love during a war raises questions about the concrete world Paz utilizes as a backdrop for this couple. Certainly, the Spanish Civil War was a war that proved compelling to an array of people seeking to fight fascism. At the same time, Paz ignored the fact that Spanish misogyny could have made his nameless woman's lovemaking particularly risky, her courage remarkable. For Paz, instead, the couple enact his suggestion that lovemaking, filled with its potential for sensual joy and/or the creation of new life, stands in profound contrast to warriors determined to maim or to kill.

Ignoring the compelling, even thorny issues a fuller grasp of gender relationships reveals, the speaker makes the couple into a pair alert to the chance—perhaps their last one—to use their bodies suggestively, even definitively. It is their opportunistic sex that emerges as a critical image, one prompting his speaker to devise a critique of the temporal life the couple's lovemaking attempted to erase.

Yet, how? The image of the couple making love was highly suggestive, even tantalizing, as the lovemaking could have been viewed as replete with an array of the sorts of emotive gestures at which Spanish and Mexican women have excelled—gestural language, generosity, enthusiasm about others. That new spatial world, though, could emerge only through a re-vision of people's previous use of space in time. That earlier world was characterized by restraint, most particularly for women. Rather than seize on the opportunity to expand that world, Paz's speaker leads readers instead to view the couple's intimacy—their private gestures occurring during a war Paz assumed to be defined by men.

How, then, did Paz understand the old life? How does he interpret that memory? Because of the couple's unique use of space in time, the speaker finds himself capable of engaging in an extensive observation of people's behavior. That observation prompts a critical rumination on the connections between time and space, one informed by the speaker's unacknowledged views on gender. Thus, within his celebration of the expansive, even explosive lovemaking couple, he turns toward another couple, one engaged in the conventional behavior of a man reading a newspaper while a woman irons.[52] Without acknowledging the contextual normalization of this gendered division of labor, the speaker instead pronounces an end of time as "there is no more time"[53] because of the emergence instead of "space, space."[54]

To be sure, people's previous use of space in time itself clamored for renovation; it was, in fact, a world characterized by constraint. The speaker leads readers toward an architecture replete with "the traps, the cells."[55] There were spaces designed, it seems, to contain longstanding institutions and customs, such as the "the confining jails, the imprisoning banks."[56] The arena was populated by an array of broken men, including "mellifluous scorpions in cap and gown,"[57] "the schoolmaster donkey,"[58] and a "favorite son of the Church."[59]

An encyclopedic array of jobs and professions, each different from the other, Paz nonetheless links the individuals who held these jobs existentially by critiquing their divisions from one another. He costumes them in putrid masks separating men from one another and from themselves.[60] They emerge as sad reminders of "the unity that we lost."[61]

Again training the speaker's gaze on the promises of the lovemaking couple, the speaker sees in them and their behavior a chance to reconfigure life itself. In that new world, slavery no longer exists; instead, slaves receive wings.[62] In that world, wine tastes as it should, as do food and water.[63] There is no marriage; instead, Héloïse's request to serve as Abelard's whore is celebrated,[64] and nothing regarding marriage's protections for women, however limited, is discussed.

Still, the continuing force and weight of the past compel the speaker to explore the earlier world filled with men encased in rancid institutions, a world replete with division. This prompts him to ponder his understanding of world history from a Mexican viewpoint. To him that history was a history of murder—indeed, one in which murder itself was celebrated.[65] Communicating that history through a tone of lamentation, the speaker picks and chooses from the world's array of victims, developing a sorrowful if exclusive list.

The Mexican world the speaker mourned was, in fact, one in which he seldom noticed women. Rather, mourning a world in time populated almost completely by men, the speaker lures readers into a history that reaches back to Agamemnon in pain.[66] It moves toward the instance when Socrates found himself "in chains,"[67] before mentioning the deaths of Brutus, Moctezuma, the French revolutionary victims.[68] Moving into the Americas, the speaker laments the deaths of Lincoln, Trotsky, and Francisco I. Madero, the man who prompted the Mexican revolution of 1910 and who was murdered during his revolutionary presidency.[69] To the speaker, this extensive list of individual deaths, all portrayed as victims, amounts to a near-infinite abuse of time itself. It is as though time has been dismembered, tragedies emptied of meaning. As he puts it, "the silence that speaks without ever speaking, does it say nothing? Are cries nothing? Does nothing happen as time passes by?"[70]

Intent on remaking himself, Paz's speaker periodically seeks a way out of the near bondage of his earlier life. Depicting himself as the voyager returning from his journey, the speaker has become a man seeking affirmation, hopeful that his new understandings of the world are acceptable. Returning to the woman he previously identified with Mexican time, he seemingly assumed she had remained unchanged. Again describing her as the embodiment of the natural world, he approaches her, suggesting that the world is refreshed "when you smile / eating an orange."[71] Once again, he has placed her in an inanimate, creaturely world, denying her speech.

Yet why is this woman placed in this silent mode? Why did the speaker refuse her speech? It strikes me that at this juncture in the poetic journey, Paz's ignorance about women and his stirring recognition about ways hierarchical governments affected men have clashed. It is as though the speaker's sudden understanding that top-down social relations hampered men was at once true but incomplete because of its refusal to notice the patriarchy embedded in that arrangement. Thus, depending on old patterns of exclusion, the speaker made the woman into a speechless accessory, a smiling orange-eater.

What captivated the speaker, as he revealed to the woman, was his new awareness of ways the former life excluded individual men. In a sudden burst of comprehension, the speaker confides crucial aspects of his new perspective on the world. Alert to the former life in which social conditions attacked men, leaving them shadowy, brittle, incapable, he asks: "When was life ever truly ours?"[72] To him life remained meaningless as long as the individual dominated. Only an understanding of the crucial need for others enabled Paz's speaker to reclaim life. To him, "there is no I, we are always us."[73]

The speaker has thus emerged as a man determined to find himself and his pathways in others. Seeking a community that could alter him, could reshape him into another sort of man, the speaker maintained that this new community is one in which his face itself emerges as "the face of us all."[74] Most importantly, he will ultimately become an individual understood as the sun itself, a sun wearing "the face of Juan,"[75] a face styled as universal, as the face of everybody.[76] A potentially inclusive vision, indeed, yet where are the faces of Phyllis, of Carmen, of the Indigenous women, the female servants, the women making tortillas, the dancers?

Turning to women to grant him permission for his new perspective on community, the speaker ignores his orange-eating companion. Instead he returns to Mary, Persephone, Heloise. To him, it is these illustrious women whom he depicts as "lunar virgin, mother of mother sea, body of the world, house of death."[77] That is, removing those women from the complicated, often messy, often deeply generous experiences characteristic of many ac- tual women's lives, the speaker instead granted them abstract control of life and death, of the natural world. That world is not one filled with the faces and experiences of actual women, but rather with those of men like the speaker and like his every man named John.[78] This speaker has, in fact, asked women to sanctify and bless what has emerged as a male-defined and male- dominated time-space.

In "Sun Stone," Paz created an extraordinary critique of Mexican men's experiences, experiences he understood as damned because of patterns of in- dividualism prompting isolation, murder, death. Understanding some of the ways personal life and political life were linked,[79] he developed an alternative approach, a new world. It was a world populated by newly freed men, men freed because they understood some of the ways in which they previously had been politically and socially excluded. Their freedom allowed them to inhabit the temporal world in more open and expansive ways.

Crucial to the speaker's discovery of that world was a journey defined by the process of wandering through a large swath of Mexican time as a partner to that temporality. This movement enabled the speaker to define and understand his experiences. It also prompted his effort to universalize his experiences marking his historico-poetic journey.

However, through his ignorance of the worlds of women, the speaker denied them an ability to participate in the journey he undertook. That refusal rendered women motionless, static. It did so because the new time-scape Paz depicted depended—as did the previous one—on female overwork, subjugation, silence. His speaker's circular journey through a universe that had entrapped all came to release him because of a partial understanding of that entrapment. His freedom from that confinement, though, depended on a temporality in which women remained enclosed within a gendered temporality in which only men would be allowed to live freely.

CHAPTER THREE

Dancing on the Sun Stone

For all the historico-poetic temporal ingenuity, all the intriguing imagery, all the exquisite and plaintive language of Paz's gendered-time-scape, the poem troubles, provokes, and disturbs. Most importantly, as I intend to discuss here, the poem, with its male author, in many ways silences and misconstrues the Mexican female and her experiences in time and space. To consider this, it is worth remembering that to guide readers through "Sun Stone," Paz developed and depended upon a male author to whom he granted the power to create a linguistic world.[1] Utilizing ideas, reflections, considerations all expressed in words on paper, Paz's author communicated a male-defined historical drama focusing on Mexican temporality. In that respect, "Sun Stone" can be understood as one version of the Mexican past, a version in which men and boys—*only* men and boys—possessed authority.

However, the combination of a male author and the focus on Mexican temporality raises concerns and questions precisely because that authoritative male author created a temporality in which female voices, considerations, views, and experiences largely went unheard. For that reason, any effort to see, hear, or consider the Michoacán girls and women prompts consideration of how Paz's author denied them voice. That is, how does this poem misconstrue and silence Michoacán female voices during this postrevolutionary period? What about that silencing invites response? How did what today is sometimes referred to as "mansplaining," "talking over," "subconscious bias" somehow animate and direct this mid-twentieth-century Mexican poem?

What has gone unquestioned has been and, in many respects, remains unquestioned is male authority in much of the primary and secondary historical documentation, in daily life, and in discussion. The consistent presence of women and girls, their minds, their accomplishments, went unseen and did so as long as both the Catholic Church and the Mexican government denied females equality before the law. By creating a narrator who accepts and reproduces that level of prejudice, by refraining from challenging that cultural perspective either poetically or historically, Paz suggests that male domination, the near invisibility and silence of females, reflected essential, undisputed experience.

This male authorial dominance itself possesses various traits, each of which silenced and erased Mexican women's and girls' temporal experiences.[2] The narrator emerged as a god. Literary expression replaced childbearing. Boys and men and *only* boys and men related to death. Male-dominated sexual experience emerged as a path to a sort of liberation reserved only for men.

To clarify these forms of erasure, it is important again to recognize that Paz's narrator often seized the female life-giving capacity and utilized it not to give birth to actual human children in time, but instead to develop the splay of words that make up the poem. With the narrator as vocal progenitor, with choice of words and deeds supplanting quests for mates, for engagement with mates, female decisions to use their bodies to contain new life, a kind of furtive theft and erasure of women's own temporal, bodily, and verbal experiences of Mexican history emerges.

As for death, which could be understood as a force equally present and potent for females and males, a force with which each gender finds itself communicating, in Paz's narrator's hands, death emerges as a male asset. At times characterizing death as a speaker, at times as experience given over only to men, Paz most consistently reveals an understanding of death as an ultimate (if ultimately annihilating) experience for men and boys. While it can seem curious to object to Paz's erasure of female experiences with death, the effect of this erasure is a refusal to dignify the female, her voice, her existential and verbal relationships with mortality.[3]

Having seized and redirected female voices in birth and in death, Paz's narrator also reveals that the Mexican experience itself, by which he means the experiences of Mexican men and boys, were troubled, entrapped by long-standing pressures to conform. Only a particular sort of behavior, a particular form of sexuality—what the speaker portrayed as sudden wartime sex—could release men from Mexican bondage. That imagistic understanding of sexual freedom itself emerges as a particular form of communication, one in which a male speaker celebrates a heterosexual experience that erases personality, erases names, erases everything about the past and the future except that of male domination of women and their forms of expression.[4]

Paz's gendered time-scape, then, ignored or misunderstood girls and women. Most particularly, Paz developed a speaker who denied female voice. He did so by denying women's and girls' abilities to engage in expository dialogue about the very Mexican temporality they uniquely experienced. There is no small irony here. After all, Paz's poem stood as a poetic response to Aztec, then modern Mexican authoritarian behavior. And yet because he refuses women and girls linguistic equality, because he apparently cannot hear their voices, he and his speaker themselves behaved in linguistic authoritarian fashions.

In the Michoacán females' requests that I discuss and assess their histories, however, the dancers and their critics granted me the opportunity to respond to that irony, to use it as an opening, an invitation for the women to reveal aspects of their array of voices, the ways their behavior itself can be understood as a form of communication in and about time. Part of my earlier responses to their invitation were to re-create and invite readers to participate in their experiences of walking into and altering history. Here I have also come to understand the women's invitations as an opportunity again to tag along through the women's historical movements, listening to the gendered language they developed, and assessing the women's changing revolutionary experiences as their own responses to the poem; as responses to a poet who failed to hear them; as the series of physical and linguistic events prompting the women to seize the poem, to make of it a new revolutionary arena, one filled with a remarkably female expression of Mexican possibilities.

Speaking of Courtship and Women

For Paz and his speaker, there was no sense of the ways northwestern Michoacán females lived, devised, or engaged worlds of physical communication. No sense of them rising before dawn, experiencing something of the physicality of partners, perhaps pondering the sun's light-to-be, its emerging heat. No actual recognition of the female physical experiences as communication. And certainly, no consideration of female sensuality or sexuality.[5]

This may be because voice and voices were themselves gendered. That is, in northwestern Michoacán, the genders experienced much about their lives distinctly because of the array of socioeconomic, ethnic, and age-based divisions there. This meant that the genders, possessing distinct experiences, likely also possessed different verbal reflections on those experiences, reflections communicated in what I understand as "gendered voice," or specific choices of words emerging through gendered temporal experiences.[6] The distinct genders drew on gendered voice precisely because women and men, girls and boys received different sorts of permission regarding topics—circumstances—about time periods during which and about which they could speak. Most particularly, in northwestern Michoacán, languages involving female involvement with courtship, sexuality, and pregnancy frequently were constrained.

In fact, for Paz and his speaker, sexuality was a male experience. It was one in which the man decided when, where, how frequently to pursue and to sleep with women. It was one in which the man confused and forgot the names of his lovers.[7] It was an experience in which men, but never women, assessed sexual experiences in time, finding them repetitious and wanting.[8]

On the other hand, in northwestern Michoacán itself, priests seemed particularly concerned about potential female sexual experience, a concern some of the villagers shared. The priests' sermons and the local gossip suggested that if girls and women experienced sexuality freely, all manner of mayhem could occur. Assaults on property? Assaults on the idea of women and girls as property? Transformation of a culture in which, simultaneously, wealth, white skin, female sexual purity, and particular ideas about female physical beauty were applauded?[9]

While Paz ignored ways that girls' and women's sensual lives were themselves forms of communication, the priests and some of the villagers seemingly viewed female sensuality as communicative, but in distressing ways. Nonetheless, everyday experience and the languages communicating that experience in northwestern Michoacán were gendered, in the sense that women and girls lived lives both with and without men and boys, while men and boys lived lives both with and without women and girls.[10]

This seemingly simple fact meant that individuals knew and experienced internal and public geography according to their gender and within the context of their previous gendered experiences. For instance, men who worked at the ranchos with other men—friends, neighbors, and cousins—shared the physical experiences of walks to and from work, experiences they lived during their work away from home. Girls and women, however, making tortillas to the light of dawn, walking the clothing to the stream, protecting the villages, may have at times experienced individuality, isolation, and pride emerging from expertise that men did not share.[11]

What, then, of languages of courtship? How can they be imagined? What did women's experiences communicate about this language? While Paz assumed that his speaker, as a man, dominated the workings of courtship, its temporality, its geography, its gendered justice, the entire arena of northwestern Michoacán female courtship experience remains tantalizing, largely because so much about it has been hidden, undescribed, leaving few documentary traces. This has meant that the sort of questions regarding a female language and experience of courtship, sexuality, and pregnancy have also gone unasked.

Nonetheless, the people I interviewed seem to have compiled what can be understood as a sort of manual of courtship.[12] Thus, the information Michoacanos shared with me included aspects of the knowledge women and men drew upon to create, consider, develop, and reproduce their relationships with one another. This information was expansive, encyclopedic, and likely necessary in an often violent world where most people were impoverished, where girls' and women's relative lack of power made information potentially crucial and protective.[13]

Thus, women learned and remembered the names of their relatives, their relatives' histories, their involvements with others, their pastimes, their abilities. They learned about neighbors and friends. Their manual responded to a series of questions focusing on material possessions. Who owned property? Who was part of the tentative middle class? Who was poor? What did friends, neighbors, and relatives possess? Where were their homes? Who participated in revolution or counterrevolution? How did women enable men to participate in military experiences? How had the revolution affected them? How pious or irreligious were they?[14]

If this manual seems deeply instrumental, it is worth considering why women's engagements with issues of courtship, marriage, and pregnancies needed to be—then and later—at once emotional, sometimes lustrous, often by necessity protective.[15] Consider the information the women and girls gathered as part of the hidden courtship manual, suggesting ways women likely related to others, about the ways, depending on instinct and context, they used language for an array of purposes. Hints suggesting that what the women told me, the information they shared, was information that at least some of them used to develop a protective, perhaps evocative language of courtship.

Again, María Enríquez's discourse about her failed relationship with Antonio Mendoza seems instructive.[16] Alert to cultural assumptions regarding the sanctity of patriarchal families complete with their supposed protections of women, Enríquez developed a language informed by magnanimity toward an array of people—her former boyfriend turned alleged sexual assailant Antonio Mendoza, his sister, her own sister, women walking to church—all of whom denied her any trace of protection. Yet rejecting a language reflecting the cultural assumption that men mattered most, Enríquez demanded respect for her own perspective, one that denied Antonio Mendoza's capacities to assault her when he insisted, "now you come with me."[17]

Enríquez not only refused him. She also reached out to others, seeking help and protection from an array of women. And while none of the women responded helpfully, as though possessing an empathic grasp regarding the sort of female experience that might have prompted them to refuse her, Enríquez declined to blame them. Indeed, her testimony revealed an understanding of women's and girls' relative powerlessness. As she pointed out, her sister assuredly had been "shocked and frightened."[18] The churchgoing women, who also refrained from helping her, likely mistook her for another woman. That woman was, Enríquez maintained, "Pachita la Loca," the "crazy woman" who, she said, frequently roamed the streets.[19]

Language of female courtship was also used in the form of advice revealing women's perspectives regarding village relationships and sociability. As Michoacán native and Cardenista teacher José Corona Nuñez reminded me, it was his mother who forbade him from associating with Tarascan Indigenous children, despite the way those children and their habits fascinated him.[20] And as Concha Méndez pointed out, in a discussion that came to focus on female village behavior, Carmen Barragán, Eloisa Barragán, and Carmen Bello were widely known as "the three beauties." "Some beauties," she continued caustically, as though to chide the women for vanity and attention only to physical appearance rather than to acts of piety.[21]

Did this language of courtship and sociability reveal—or at least suggest—ways that women defined meeting places? Does it discuss why and how they chose their partners or enabled themselves to be chosen? Does it in fact amount to an unwritten sort of courtship primer filled with language and silence, information and absences, the very sort of useful and yet inadequate information that could both help or injure girls and women?

Because males and females lived lives at once united by gender and home lives and segregated by gender and work lives, the manual I suggest here, the one I am describing and defining, reminds me that even meeting potential partners could have been challenging. At the same time, census material revealing that women and men did in fact encounter one another, conduct sexual relationships, and populate the area compels me, at least, to inquire into the ways young women and men might have discovered one another. For instance, on occasions when young men worked with their fathers on the ranches and women allowed their daughters to walk with them to take lunch to the men, a young man might have caught a young woman's eye.[22] Then, too, young men and women might notice one another in church, or in the new coeducational public schools.[23] The frequent experiences walking on the plaza after dinner, the very place Méndez understood as the arena where villagers congregated, greeted one another, shared gossip, might also have provided matchmaking opportunities.[24]

What, then, do languages focusing on or prompting intimacy reveal? While census materials demonstrate that men frequently impregnated specific women, this statistical information says nothing about the languages of physical and emotional intimacy women and men likely developed. Nor does census material mention that until menopause, sexual intimacy provided—or threatened—frequent possibilities of pregnancies, creating specific physical and psychological risks and pleasures for women but not for men. Creating, in fact, deep female physical dialogues—those surrounding sexuality, those surrounding women's pregnancies that, though unwritten or undiscovered by scholars, continue to intrigue.[25]

Women's participation in courtship and its consequences were themselves, it seems, specific languages filled with gesture, uncertainties, decisions, desire and tenderness. That is, the women likely developed emotive languages as vast and enthralling, at times as surprising, at times as routinized as their day-to-day experiences. Flirtatious languages, languages discussing decisions about when, where, how to court, experiences of lovemaking and its multifaceted languages. And the tactile vocabularies of pregnancy, vocabularies known in full only to the women who created them in relationship with their children-to-be that the women depended on their bodies to contain.[26]

When Michoacán Girls and Women Liberated Speech

The revolutionary women's leagues, the brainstorm of Zamora agrarian leader Juan Gutiérrez, played a number of transformative roles in the re-creation of postrevolutionary Mexico. As I've previously discussed, women used these leagues to create and amplify some of the revolutionary men's anticlerical and prorevolutionary positions.[27] In addition, as I hope to reveal here, the women used the league meetings as backdrops against which girls and women devised and orchestrated what emerged as previously unknown vocal arrangements and as previously unknown relationships with Mexico's gendered temporality.

Further, to follow the women's geographic pathways to the meetings allows deeper understanding of ways that women's gendered relationships with the physical settings altered the possibilities that geography often contained. The ways, too, that when upon receiving invitations to the league meetings women likely found themselves compelled—or able—to rearrange their schedule of chores and of their movements through the village. While the area, including its paths, roadways, and streams, previously and persistently hosted women carrying clothing to launder, or young girls befriending one another, or courtships-in-the-making, now women and girls found themselves creating additional territorial uses. Considering the combination of uncertainty and surprise informing the female revolutionary gathering, the women walking may have wondered if or how the meeting might further affect their schedules, their perspectives. Step by step they found their ways to meet with other girls and women in previously untried and thus unknown ways.[28]

Likely arriving at a sala, a front room owned by one of the men referred to as an "agrarista," or a person who accepted a piece of governmental land,[29] the girls and women likely were greeted by the agrarista's wife. Though for some of the women being there would have been novel, the place itself possessed a history, one in which walls, floor, and ceiling connected to those who lived and visited there. In a village as gregarious and gossip-filled as Ario, some of the women may have known something about that spatial history. All would have known their presence there amounted to novel experiences of time and space.[30]

It was as though that room, that space, absorbed expectation and excitement. It was as though it became a character awaiting new experiences of voice in time, new characters speaking in novel ways. And yet, how? What do their political experiences in league meetings say about gendered voice? About the women's use of space in time? About, in fact, their response to the ways Paz ignored and silenced them, the church demanding their modesty, their demure behavior? How did women there begin to alter spatial geography and sentiment? How will what they are about, again, to say respond to the ways Paz silenced them, made them invisible, and the fashions in which the church demanded that women behave modestly, chastely, demurely?[31]

To be sure, previously girls and women had related to space, usually spaces owned by men or other male-dominated institutions, in multiple ways. Some of those ways were ambulatory; some were deferential to men, in the sense that women performed an array of tasks for men and boys in outdoor spaces, in clerical spaces, in homes. Some, too, were intimate, as only females found themselves giving the spaces of their wombs over to potential new life. What united these spatial arrangements were, again, top-down, male-defined power relationships, relationships often communicated and experienced verbally.

While I have assessed the political novelty of Gutiérrez's political invitation to women and the original ways women responded to that invitation, what also emerged as new during this postrevolutionary period was the fashion in which property itself suddenly emerged as a sort of arena prompting female redefinitions.[32] Understandings of the places owned by others where only women cooked, cleaned, brought water, tended men and children, subtly began to shift. Building on their conversational customs, the array of personal knowledge they had accumulated, the women began filling the room itself with a new level of discourse. Where previously only men received breaks enabling them to relax and explore ways of using time, in the meetings the women claimed permission to use time and space to devise a new political language.[33]

Thus, along with their political connotations, the league meetings can be understood as temporal instances in which women were encouraged to use time and space anew; to fill space with female, and only female, presence.[34] While previously I focused on the women's league as part of a grassroots resistance movement to Cárdenas's presidential revolutionary approaches, a focus on the league women's historical connections to time and space reveals ways the meetings emerged as opportunities for women—only women—to understand their voices in time and space in original fashions.

In particular, some of the women at the league meetings revealed a recognition of the male clerical tendencies to seize temporal space not only to undermine revolutionary objectives, including the land reform and the public schooling, but also to minimize female presence. In that regard, while the leaders of the leagues certainly utilized the anticlerical language male revolutionaries had developed, when female liga leaders like Matilde Anguiano and Maria Loreto Pacheco experimented with this language, its effect was at once to critique the church's counterrevolutionary tendencies, and to respond to clerical tendencies to undermine female speech.

For Loreto Pacheco and Anguiano, that sort of gendered silencing proved unacceptable. Not only did they organize a letter-writing campaign against the illegal presence of priests, a campaign they may well have discussed in liga meetings, but they also used the meetings themselves as backdrops for their new, experimental voices. Voices they used to rebuke those women who spent their time seeking an illegal priest, time during which, as Pacheco put it, the women "engaged in deviation and fanaticism."[35] And voices they used to "turn against the church," as Ario villager Rafael Ochoa González put it.[36]

These women's language functioned in an array of ways. In their public critiques of individuals seeking to undermine the progress of a male-dominated revolution, women certainly collaborated with revolutionary men who lacked verbal, gestural, and social connections to women. And the liga women did more. If previously scholars have refrained from historicizing the existence and journeys female voices have traveled, if Paz eliminated Mexican women's consistent and ever-changing relationships to time,[37] there in Ario, on specific afternoons when the revolutionary women's leagues met, some women used their voices to create new verbal possibilities, possibilities at once creating and engaging revolutionary possibilities, and, too, creating female capacities to engage revolution.

The women thus amplified Mexican revolutionary and postrevolutionary experience. Most particularly, by treating their own and other women's behavior as political speech, relevant to the re-creation of postrevolutionary Mexico and its institutional life, women made female language itself into a series of politicized acts. In doing so, the women thus amplified considerations of the Mexican revolution and its history, one often understood as only devised and defined by men whose battlefield behavior, and nothing else, defined historical temporality.[38]

Speaking through the Flames

For many Ario villagers, the dance before the altar in the church emerged as an expression of transgressive behavior. At the same time, the dance can also be viewed as a political expression of female movement in time. How, then, might that dance also have spoken directly to Paz? That is, how was the dance a reflection of female language? To understand more about the multidimensional meanings of the dance, it may be worth thinking about the Michoacán dance yet again, seeking out the fashions in which Ario women used their temporal experiences in the church in communication with Paz.

While women in the leagues developed and practiced new revolutionary languages, it appears that the new revolutionary uses of time itself threatened some of the conservative Ario villagers. In particular, the presence of the leagues combined with the land reform and the revolutionary schooling concerned the conservatives in Ario.[39] As though these villagers so feared the potential range and reach of the liga women's languages, they responded by furtively entering the church. And as though protective of their senses of the past, fearful of women's engagements with a future they found threatening, the men seized images of Jesus, of some of the saints, and of the Virgin Mary, icons reflecting aspects of the traditional Catholicism practiced there.[40]

Soon after, however, Ario revolutionary men entered the church where priests had promoted a status quo that muted female voices and honored an economic realm that undermined most men's economic well-being.[41] It may have been that the revolutionary men who entered the church that day understood the ways religious iconography itself had reflected the view that had enabled only some voices to be heard, while silencing others. Certainly, the men assessed the contents of the room. Looking around, they encountered several icons the conservative men had inadvertently left behind.[42]

Scooping up the icons that themselves reflected a gendered temporal history, the men took them home.[43] Back home, they encountered their wives, women who may have continued to use time to serve men and children while also considering new possibilities of temporal experimentation provided by the ligas. Initially, though, the women likely behaved in conventional fashion, using time to prepare food for their men and children, then cleaning up while the men enjoyed siestas.

It would be after those naps that the men invited women to experience time in novel ways. Asking their mates and daughters to join them, the men carried the iconography to the village plaza. Once there, the men and women used what emerged as a temporal interlude to seek out wood, arrange it, and then build a bonfire on the plaza. After the embers blazed, men and women tossed the icons into the fire.[44]

What could this mean? How had the women who participated in the torching communicated? In Mexico's extensive history of battles between liberals and conservatives, anticlerical behavior was not unusual. In northwestern Michoacán, though, such behavior tended to be gendered, with women frequently embracing Catholic piety far more than men did. And yet that evening, in that plaza, the Ario women used their bodies and psyches to make physical comments on elements of longstanding Catholic ritual, rituals that previously had been used to prompt the silencing of women. Then, too, the women used their bodies in time in ways suggesting a commentary on "Sun Stone."

It was as though because of their experiences with temporality—their presences and futures taken up by chores at home and in the village—because of the new ideas, thoughts, and feelings emerging in the revolutionary language with which they experimented in the leagues, the women claimed permission to experiment with different approaches to spiritual life. If on the one hand, the priests' threats to excommunicate men who accepted plots of land from the revolutionary government and parents who sent their children to the revolutionary schools proved unsettling, on the other hand, women may have remembered the comforts of prayer and religious celebrations.[45] Assuredly, their men likely had particular reasons for concern about some of the priests' close connections to landlords who mistreated them.[46] And certainly, women's understanding of the church can be understood as the regard a person might have for the sort of private protective space prayer—and its celebration—provides.

Within that context, the women's engagement in the saints' burning hints at a particular sort of gendered declaration, one suggesting a willingness to explore a world in which elements of Catholicism, or elements of matter that women previously used protectively, even lovingly, could be reconsidered and engaged in new, provocative fashions—as though the women were experimenting with a new temporality in which they communicated historically, even poetically in unprecedented ways.

Dancing on the Sun Stone

After the icons burned, charring memories in the air above, men invited the women away from the plaza. At that point, the men invited the women to accompany them into what had been the church building. A place that had revealed itself, in part, through its longstanding and historical ornaments, its images of Jesus, an array of saints, an image of La Purísima, the regional patron saint adorned in silk and crowned in gold.

Agreeing to accompany their men into the church, the women walked inside only to encounter a different sort of arena. A space where popular musicians were playing and a place where their men invited them to dance. Upon agreeing to dance, the women began moving in that space in time. The political originality of their dance itself had its part in the grassroots Michoacán movement that reconstituted the Cardenista efforts to at once alter their cultures and their daily experiences.[47]

At the same time, the women's dance can be understood as a fuller, more suggestive form of communication regarding temporality. Indeed, their gestures exemplified their multiple historical vocabularies, including those sensual vocabularies that populated northwestern Michoacán, carrying lives from their wombs into the outer world. Phrases reflecting their bodily experiences, crouching, shaping the food that nurtured their families. Sentences that had defined and determined courtship. Complete proclamations reflecting their intellectual and emotional experiences in the women's revolutionary leagues.

And that night, in that church-that-was, the women altered yet more by dancing. By dancing then and there, the women developed new temporal and physical relationships to bodies and church. They re-created what church could be. What church could be as the women inhabited that space, then, there, as no one had before. As women used bodies long misunderstood, misconstrued, limited, to communicate, to develop and express physical language that previously had not existed. [48]

Watching them, hovering close enough to observe what they did, and on this page do again, I see women using their bodies speaking to a church and a clerical realm that had depended on their modesty, chastity, silence. But I also see them speaking to, talking back to the Paz of his "Sun Stone." By imagining their presence, by observing them again, it is possible to see them using their bodies in time to defy the ways Paz diminished female temporal experiences.

It is possible to watch their movements through space as a defiance of that death stone, an evocation of life in time.

To watch them there is to encounter women responding to the poet and to the other men who denied or minimized their presence in time. That is, in their dance that night, the women used sensibilities filled with the array of temporal voices, memories, to communicate in ways Paz never saw, considered, or heralded. While part of what they did by dancing was to demonstrate and amplify a power they created by seizing permission, to communicate to and about the church in new ways, the women also used their bodies to reveal—through bending here, bowing there, cuddling the light in the room—the limitation of Paz's focus on death.

Sun stone? Death stone? A temporal image enabling Paz to generalize about Mexico's long historical patterns and, in doing so, to eliminate the women's presence. Yet there that night, step by step, breath by breath, the women revealed their consistent relationships to a lively sort of time, an engagement with time brought to life precisely because of their multiple forms of experiencing temporality, communicating their experiences with time itself, with life itself.

In many ways, the Mexican revolution, that series of male-dominated outbursts made possible by female overwork, focused on claiming or reclaiming property. Yet the women that night in the Ario church created a distinct approach. Against all those who ignored them, they presented themselves. Against the poet who sanctified death and then found release and redemption in a sexuality in which women and their desires remained unseen and unmet, the dancing women displayed something of the complexities of touch, of feeling.

Within and against a church-state rivalry, in response to a poet who denied their voices, the women that night reclaimed and developed a new temporality, a new vocabulary. Seizing the death stone and bringing it to life, the women defined a new distinctive revolutionary time-scape: a place and a way to dance their lives, to speak their lives, to communicate the revolutionary possibilities of lives in time created by, alert to, and responsive to the evocative and gestural voices of girls and women.

CHAPTER FOUR

The Dance of Paz's Legacy

Initially I hoped to write a concluding chapter in which the Michoacán dancers and other Mexican women could dance with Octavio Paz's legacy, one
much created by his poetics and his twin cultural studies, *The Labyrinth of
Solitude*[1] and *The Other Mexico: Critique of the Pyramid.*[2] Such an approach
seemed possible because of Paz's longstanding and stated desire for a fairer
Mexico, the very sort of approach the Michoacán dancers embodied and
shared.

Yet dance often requires partners' respectful understandings of one another. It is a sort of partnership that Paz's unconscious bias against Mexican girls and women throws into question. This is largely because Paz determined that the Mexico that most interested him, the Mexico that most
mattered, was male Mexico. Moreover, Paz's approach to the social issues he
addressed in both *The Labyrinth of Solitude* and *The Other Mexico: Critique of
the Pyramid* was itself inadequate, precisely because of his incapacity to fully
and fairly view Mexican history from a perspective that included females.[3]

Instead, in both studies, Paz casts Mexican men and boys as Mexico's central political actors. Thus, in *The Labyrinth of Solitude* he traces Mexican machismo not to the Spanish conqueror of Mexico Hernan Cortés, but rather
to his Indigenous mistress La Malinche's decision to sleep with him.[4] And
while Paz's *The Other Mexico* emerges as a critique of dehumanizing modern
Mexican governance, Paz's continuing incapacity or refusal to consider how
that governance affected females also defines that text.

Nonetheless, Paz's approach, what I view as the dance of his legacy, compels attention for various reasons. Paz emerged as a self-styled and internationally acclaimed Mexican spokesperson; his cultural studies reveal his
understanding of those he understood as his fellow Mexicans.[5] His critique

of fellow Mexicans, too, suggests a courageous attempt to understand his country. Turning to historical sources regarding the Mexican past that themselves largely eliminated females, Paz used those studies as a primer, revealing the sources of Mexican boys' and men's behavior patterns. At the same time, Paz's incapacity—or refusal—to notice the multiple ways Mexican girls and women have experienced and helped create Mexico leaves him as an individual poet and critic mired in a solitary labyrinth of his making.

To understand the dance of Paz's legacy calls for an approach sensitive to his inadequate grasp of Mexican gender relations, one alert to the fact that the very Mexican girls and women Paz failed to see or acknowledge proved crucial to the making and reproduction of Mexican history. To trace the dance of Paz's legacy, then, is to observe a dance in which he failed to engage women as full partners. It is to question his solitary illusion. It is to wonder about the sources of his views, most especially his views on gender. It is to enter a historico-poetic conversation and interrogation of both the originality and the inadequacy of his approaches.

La Malinche as Mother of Mexican Solitude

Paz's cultural study, *The Labyrinth of Solitude*, emerges as an effort to assess and critique what he viewed as the psychology of the Mexican. While individuals with a credulous or hopeful view might understand his topic to be the psychology of all Mexicans, the central object of Paz's concern was the psychology of Mexican men and boys, not that of Mexican women and girls.[6] In particular, Paz sought to explain what he understood as an array of behavioral traits displayed by Mexican men and boys, traits including hypersensitivity, exaggerated courtesy, refusal to reveal one's deepest personal traits to others, and thoughtless determination to resolve differences violently.[7]

If many Mexican men understood Cortés's Aztec mistress and interpreter La Malinche as the source of Indigenous Mexico's military loss to the sixteenth-century Spanish conquerors, Paz understood that tryst slightly differently. To him, the widespread male shame that Mexican men experienced because of their view of La Malinche as the woman whose affair with Cortés betrayed fellow Mexicans was itself problematic for Mexican men.[8] In particular, La Malinche's experience as Cortés's mistress not only made her "la chingada," ("the fucked one"), but also—in the minds of many—the female parent of generations of children possessing the cultural "stain" of mixed ethnic ancestry. In addition, Paz considered La Malinche the source of Mexican men's tendencies to wear self-denying masks, to in fact live within the labyrinth of solitude.[9]

While Paz seemingly blamed Mexican men for seeing La Malinche in such limited ways, he himself determined that her decision to sleep with Cortés was one she freely and voluntarily made. As he put it, "it is true that she gave herself voluntarily to the conquerors."[10] That is, in what appears to be an effort to enable La Malinche to possess and to bear responsibility for her fate, Paz refrains from understanding Mexican history and, most particularly, the multiple worlds in which she lived from her perspective.

This view that La Malinche freely slept with Cortés informed Paz's failure to think about her and her life from a perspective alert to the vast gendered physical and psychological challenges she confronted within the power-drenched worlds in which she lived. After all, these challenges consistently made La Malinche's decisions highly contingent. And to understand Mexico's gendered history, it is worth attempting to puzzle them out.

For example, a perspective alert to La Malinche herself would see her as a crucial Mexican whose choices consistently were limited because of her gender, and, once the Spaniards arrived in Mexico, because of her ethnic background. While La Malinche left no written documentation regarding her experiences, the Spanish conqueror Bernal Díaz de Castillo pointed out that her parents relinquished her to Mayan-speaking traders from Tabasco.[11] They enslaved her. When the Spaniards arrived, the Tabasco Mayan-speaking natives gave La Malinche and an array of other women up to the Spaniards as war booty.[12]

Within that context, how did La Malinche experience her life? From her perspective, what could this persistent use of her body and being according to the whims, desires, and demands of others have meant? Why did she decide to reveal her linguistic abilities to the Spaniards?[13] Why did she sleep with Cortés? What informed her decisions to avoid violence, including violence against herself? What led her instead to use language as a key resource in her connections with the Spaniards?

Paz's notion that La Malinche drew on her free will when she agreed to sleep with Cortés blinded him to the series of contexts in which La Malinche operated, all much informed by male domination. Further, Paz's view enabled him (like the Mexican men he critiques) to hold Malinche singlehandedly responsible for the consequences of the Spanish conquest of the Aztecs. It enables him to ignore Cortés himself, his Tlaxcalan Indigenous allies whose fury against the Aztecs enabled the Spaniards to conquer militarily, even the male translator who with Malinche told the Spaniards what Indigenous Mexicans may have said.[14]

Limiting his interest in La Malinche to her sexual experiences and the bastard child she had with Cortés, Paz understood the child emerging from those experiences as the source of the long misogynist fury he imputes to Mexican men.[15] What is highly curious, even worrisome, is Paz's failure to problematize La Malinche's decisions and thus to begin to see more about the Mexican ancestor she was. It is particularly startling that Paz fails to see and assess her linguistic talent and to recognize the scope of the decisions she made. After all, La Malinche decided not to evade the European strangers, or to respond to them—or to herself—in overtly violent ways. Her choice of language rather than violence suggests that she created—or participated in—a practice that contrasted with the Spanish warriors' ethnocide. Failing to note this, Paz left himself entrapped within his own labyrinthine thinking.

Octavio Paz and the Masculinization of the Mexican Revolution

For Paz, the Mexicans (who must be understood as Mexican men and boys) were masked, filled with an array of hidden, highly expressive emotions and urges.[16] For Paz, it was during the 1910 Mexican Revolution that Mexican males expressed those urges. After all, he saw that revolution as a series of outbursts through which Mexican men—only men—relinquished their masks and emerged, revealing the authentic face of Mexico, a face he saw as the "brutal, resplendent face of death and fiestas, of gossip and gunfire, of celebration and love (which is rape and pistol shots)."[17] For Paz, the revolution amounted to a militarized upheaval in which Mexican men's behavior provided almost redemptive release.[18]

While many scholars of the revolution have also seen redemptive qualities in the revolution-turned-civil war, many of these scholars have understood the sources of that revolution as socioeconomic and political, and more recently, cultural. For such scholars, the fashions in which the 1876–1910 dictatorship of Porfirio Díaz threatened local economies and self-governance prompted the widespread array of local outbursts that together defined the revolution. And some of the more recent scholarly approaches to the revolution have included gender within the larger cultural dimensions of this revolution. Viewing culture as a people's complex, contentious, and changing world view, these scholars have focused on specific ways that people's cultures defined both the revolutionary outbursts and the series of revolutionary alliances they made.[19]

Paz, however, depended on a world view linking Freud's concern with instinct and Marx's with material conditions. This enabled him to consider the Morelos revolutionary Emiliano Zapata as the most crucial of Mexican revolutionaries.[20] To Paz, Zapata was not the ruffian earlier scholars and journalists saw.[21] Rather, he and the guerrilla warriors he organized revealed Mexican personality and behavior in the starkest and most authentic ways. Indeed, to Paz, the Zapatista peasants of Morelos shed Mexican masks when they made war, murdered, and raped.[22]

Paz not only celebrated Zapatista violence and rapacity. Celebrating Zapatista men as heroic, Robin Hood–like individuals, Paz gloried in their uprisings, fueled by desire to recover their stolen property, political rights, and personal dignity. He saw their refusal to accept the national power they won militarily as a mark of their dedication to their traditional village-centered pasts.[23] To Paz, the murders, the thefts, the rapes themselves revealed the depth of Zapatista—and indeed of Mexican men's identities.

Paz, however, placed Zapata and his movement within a gendered vacuum. The revolution that Paz saw and mythologized was only a portion of the revolution that Mexicans experienced. By celebrating Zapatista democracy as the crucial path out of the solitary labyrinth, Paz celebrated—without noticing it—a restoration of economic and political rights, but only for men. Paz's consistent failures to see women's involvement in Mexican political culture frequently blinded him to Mexican women's engagement in the country's extensive history. Most especially, Paz refrained from noticing the fashions that Mexican governmental power often reflected male struggles to assert power over females, a sort of power based on coercion, persuasion, and frequently resulting in widespread female overwork.

While Paz's failure to notice women's engagement in revolution might appear to be a limited or one-time lapse, here he revealed an inability to imagine what he failed to see. He revealed a material cultural blindness to the fact that, without the historical patterns of Mexican women and girls' behavior, the Mexican revolution would not have taken place as it did. Further, while scholars have well described the vastness of Mexican revolutionary geography in regional terms,[24] to consider female engagement with the revolution, it is also worth thinking about what can be referred to as the revolution's emotive architecture, a revolutionary geography that included bedrooms, kitchens, paths to the streams, the streams themselves, and the cornfields.

It was upon this gender-inclusive territory, this gender-inclusive idea regarding revolutionary geography where women enabled men to leave home to fight, and from which women themselves left home to fight.[25] Upon this geography it was women who prepared food for children, men, hungry warriors. It was also women who maintained households and cared for children.

While Mexican women's roles in defining and experiencing the contours of the revolution proved extensive, Paz limited his perspective of the revolution to a conventional view. The revolutionary violence Paz celebrated was based on the idea that a new world can only emerge through men's violent, murderous destruction of the old. It was a perspective that celebrated men brave enough to use their bodies against other bodies to communicate in the most vivid ways, who was to live and who to die. It was also a perspective that remained aloof from Mexican girls and women. By ignoring female intellectual and tactile involvement in issues of life and death, Paz suggested in an ahistorical fashion that Mexican women were to be excluded from issues involving mortality.

Paz's masculinization of the Mexican revolution depended on an isolated, entrapped, and ahistorical view of Mexican gender relations. It was a view that ignored Mexico's history of gender relations, the ways that, notwithstanding extensive male domination in Mexico, men and women, boys and girls often depended on one another in an array of ways. Further, by ignoring the gendered contours of the revolution, Paz ignored the vast gendered promises the revolution offered to men and to women, promises hinting that perhaps in the homes and on the battlefields, new Mexican gender relations themselves would emerge, relationships prompting an escape from the labyrinth.

The Other, Other Mexico

The year 1968 was a year of international citizen outbursts, and in Mexico, too, an array of mostly urban students organized, requesting that the post-revolutionary Mexican government communicate with them as citizens. In response to the student request, Mexican governmental agents slaughtered student after student.[26] On learning about the killing, Octavio Paz resigned from his position as Mexican ambassador to India. In addition, in direct response to the slaughter, Paz wrote *The Other Mexico: Critique of the Pyramid*, his second study of Mexican national character.[27]

For Paz, the source of the slaughter was a longstanding view of the world in top-down, hierarchical terms, an understanding that informed Mexican governmental structures. Mexico's postrevolutionary government inherited and reproduced the understanding of government. As before, Paz found the origins of that approach to government in that of the Aztecs, which demonstrated Aztec failure to nurture human life.[28] To Paz, notwithstanding the revolutionary hopes of Mexicans who participated in the revolution, postrevolutionary Mexican governments failed to serve the Mexican majority. And to Paz, the late twentieth-century result of that failure was the creation of two very distinct Mexicos.

To Paz, one Mexico, the visible one, was the modern, postrevolutionary Mexico filled with an array of people, some wealthy, some poor, some Indigenous, some mestizo, but all subject to a rationalized governing authority.[29] The other Mexico to which Paz referred, however, was to a respect to be understood in concrete terms, referring to Mexico's long development of a wealthy, well-fed, well-educated population, supported by Mexicans who found themselves impoverished, poorly fed, and poorly educated. Of more significance to Paz, though, was a version of Mexico to be understood metaphysically. It was the Mexico Paz described as "really other," as a "submerged and repressed" series of attitudes that reappear in modern Mexico.[30] That other Mexico was a hidden Mexico fashioned by long-ago attitudes toward life and particularly toward death. To Paz, that Mexico, though submerged, lived within the psyches of Mexican men and proved defining. Indeed, it was the Mexico where Aztec torture and annihilation flourished. To Paz, the 1968 massacre revealed that that level of inhumanity persisted.

While there is considerable sensitivity to Paz's view regarding Mexico's longstanding democratic failures and their potential causes, Paz's approach proved to be unaware of what I here refer to as "the other, other Mexico." That is, Paz noticed some of the divisions characterizing Mexican history: those based on ethnicity, those based on class, and those he understood as viewed on a murderous reproduction of the Aztec perspective. At the same time, however, Paz failed to notice the existence, the workings, or the Mexico produced by yet another division, that of gender.

Paz's refusal to understand, see, hear Mexican females, their historical conditions and experiences, their lives in 1968, startles. It may be because Paz lived during a period in which his everyday experiences in home, family, and society were those in which females themselves lived lives that men scarcely noticed. It may also be that he learned to pay limited attention to those lives because they were experienced by females rather than by males. Or it may be because nothing in Paz's experience prompted him actually to see, to ponder Mexican structural divisions based on gender, and the longstanding implications of those divisions.

What, then, is this "other, other Mexico"? Who were some of the people who populated it? What conditions did they experience in the postrevolutionary period? And how did females take part in the 1968 resistance movement?

While the other, other Mexico was female Mexico, what characterized its otherness was Mexico's longstanding patriarchy, its series of institutions reflecting views that men mattered more than women. What makes this other, other Mexico remarkable, as late as 1968, is the fact that both during the revolutionary and the postrevolutionary periods, many Mexicans, including women, clamored for recognition of their lives and contributions. Yet, as late as 1968, many Mexicans, and most particularly Mexican females, in many ways continued to go unseen, unnoticed, and unheard.

Although Paz said nothing about Mexico's widespread employment of female domestic labor, studies revealed that by 1970, 19 percent of Mexican females served as domestic servants in private homes; no single source of male employment proved to be so extensive.[31] Female servants' tasks included some of the tasks long assigned to mothers, including cooking, cleaning, and taking care of children. Within that context, it was female servants' labor that often enabled both men and women to work outside the home. At the same time, however, women's experience of that work proved to be confining in an array of fashions, including the fact that the terms of these women's work drew them from their own homes and families and compelled them to work for long hours for minimal pay.[32] Often their shelter amounted to any unused, untended corner of the employer's home; often they went poorly compensated, or compensated only by leftover food. Often, too, men in the family harassed and abused them.[33]

While the revolution that came to northwestern Michoacán affected much, it refrained from undermining the widespread practice of female servitude. Indeed, just to scratch the surface of these women's lives is to view elements of the fragile, the confining, and at times the perilous qualities of these women's employment experience. Even some of the Purépecha Indigenous servants in postrevolutionary northwestern Michoacán, who were in some ways appreciated by their employers, faded into near social invisibility. It appears that that invisibility was expected of them, a condition of their employment. It was as though these women were hired to become, to impersonate the tasks they performed.[34]

For instance, the widow Suzanna de Sierra employed a Purépecha woman named Esperanza to live in the home and to perform an array of tasks. She rose before the dawn to heat bath water for her employer and for the employer's family members. She cooked. She cleaned the home. She tended children and grandchildren. She mopped up unexpected rainwater from the front room. Yet, according to de Sierra, "I had to let Esperanza go."[35] That is, there came a time when de Sierra could no longer afford to pay the servant's wages. Through no fault of her own, Esperanza lost her job.

Ario resident Maria Elena Verduzco de Peña also employed a Purépecha woman to work for her. In this case, Verduzco de Peña depended on the servant to assist her in her small business of creating Catholic ceremonial regalia that Verduzco de Peña sold. Likely because the servant was younger than she was and thus able to see more clearly, Verduzco de Peña required the servant to fabricate artificial pearls to be attached to the ceremonial outfits. Thus, the young woman dipped her hands into a pot of clay, selected a small portion of that clay, and shaped it into a pearl-to-be. Then she dipped a brush into enamel and painted the pearl, which she subsequently attached to the clothing. [36]

Concepción Méndez was the Ario resident who discussed the ways that women's workload proved limiting enough and confining enough that she understood cooking, cleaning, and ironing clothes to be women's "destiny." Yet as Méndez also recognized, while no men experienced such a "destiny," she and her sister were able to evade those "predestined" tasks assigned to females. As she pointed out, because her family had the means to hire a servant who performed such tasks, she and her sister were able to leave home, attend mass, and visit with their relatives.[37]

And though Paz failed to notice, women who rose up to participate in the 1968 resistance movement were themselves inhabitants of this other, other Mexico. What impresses is the female protesters' political range. While both women and men protested the Mexican government's lack of transparency, for women the government represented and reproduced institutional failures to reflect female concerns. Then, too, some of the women experienced the movement itself as an incubator for what would be their emerging participation in organized Mexican feminism.[38]

The women who resisted in 1968 also remain striking because of their political and sociological distinctions. Certainly, in some cases, their experiences of male domination in the movement itself prompted them to become feminists. Other women like Ana Ignacia Rodriguez and Roberta Avendaño ("Tita") Martínez made the 1968 student movement their own, giving time, ideas, and commitment.[39] The movement also included unlikely female participants from wealthy families, like the young women from Mexico City's prosperous Polanco district who borrowed their family cars to drive fellow movement participants to meetings.[40] Tragically, the movement included women like Margarita Nolasco and Rafaela Salmeron de Contreras, whose consistent and unsuccessful quests to find their tortured and murdered siblings and children throughout Mexico City's morgues, jails, and governmental offices permanently transformed their lives and Mexican history itself.[41]

The cultural assumptions about Mexican gender relations informing both his 1950 *Labyrinth of Solitude* and *The Other Mexico: Critique of the Pyramid* suggest Paz's continuing cultural blindness to worlds in which Mexican women and girls lived. That is, in both of these studies, Paz failed to observe that Mexican society and culture were patriarchal. Instead, his focus in both studies is on a Mexico populated by and defined by males. When women emerge, their experiences are treated as unusual, parenthetical, barely significant in the scope of Mexican society and culture. Paz, then, simply failed to see, hear, feel, or understand the other, other Mexico, the world in which Mexican girls and women lived.

Yet it was those females who systematically experienced a Mexico that confined and mistreated them because of their gender. As systematically, Mexican women of all ethnicities, classes, and sexual persuasions experienced and affected the world in which they lived. They were the citizens of this alternative, other Mexico. They were women whose experiences all were tinged by Mexico's long democratic inadequacies. They were also women whose experiences within those parameters shaped and colored Mexico's other, another Mexico.

This Mexico was populated by an array of diverse women like La Malinche, whose linguistic genius reshaped Mexico. The many women whose domestic overwork enabled Mexican men and women to work outside of their homes were also part of this Mexico. So, too, were the 1968 female protesters, whose protest was against a government at once hierarchical and patriarchal. Together, these women at once personified an array of experiences distinct from those of men. And together, these women animated a Mexico Paz failed to imagine.

The Dance of Paz's Legacy

The dance of Paz's legacy contains an array of movements. They include his use of language, including poetic language, to understand Mexican history and what he viewed as its cultural underpinnings. They include his concerns to assess and critique a Mexico that lacked a democratic institutional framework. Crucially, they include the view he elaborated in his poem "Sun Stone," a view that claimed that the murderous Mexican temporality of the sun stone could be altered through Mexican men's critique of that past. Ironically, however, Paz's legacy also includes his consistent failure to notice Mexican female history, including that of the Michoacán women who, that night in the church, demonstrated a far more open approach to Mexican temporality.

To consider the scope of what the dancers did, and to view the dance in democratic terms, it is useful to remember that the sun stone, which Paz believed affected all Mexicans, was a symbol that could have had limited or no meaning at all in parts of Mexico where Aztecs and their descendants did not live or dominate. That is, the actual historical sun stone existed in a physical area far from the lives of the mestiza Michoacán women dancers, whose ancestors likely were a combination of Spaniards, Creoles, and Purépecha Indigenous people. The Michoacán women's worlds had been highly religious Catholic worlds where La Purísima served as the patron saint. As inhabitants of temporal worlds in which their survival depended on their development of an array of relationships with more powerful individuals and, later, as inhabitants of revolutionary worlds in which they experimented with more democratic practices, Mexican girls and women experienced realities about which Paz knew nothing.

Thus, to place the women within the confines of Paz's thinking about gender and democracy makes little sense. Rather, it is worth seeing the women's experiences as responses to his perspective. After all, "Sun Stone" and his cultural studies are informed by Paz's yearning for patriarchal democracy. How different his legacy could have been, had he noticed the women in the church that night, as they embodied an alternative to a legacy that refused to see them, to consider them.

Indeed, the women's own legacy, the one Paz evaded, prompts a return to that former church with the women themselves. To accompany them is to hear the backyard Mexican musicians playing secular music for all who entered. It is to see the women not only as partners to the men, as mothers and daughters. It is also to see them as their movements drew on pasts, including their gender-exclusive workaday pasts, their religious experiences, their recent practice of democratic social relations in the women's leagues. It is to see their dance in highly expansive ways as the women Soledad Barragán, Carmen Barragán, and Carmen Bueno included men and other women in their celebration. As they then and there used their bodies to communicate about an array of Mexican experiences—including those of the sun stone—that included and excluded them. As they used their bodies in time, there and then, to embody a Mexican democratic revolutionary practice, one that included women, girls, men, boys—all Mexicans.

Dancing with the Dancers

To again ponder the significance of the dancers' gendered worlds, their gendered voices, the continuing meanings of their dance within a more recent context, it is important to think about the crucial connections between female voice, presence, and resistance. Indeed, it makes sense to link the dancers' multilayered forms of communication in the church that night in 1937 with those of more contemporary Mexican and other Latin American women resisting femicide, including women singing, "it wasn't my fault, not where I was, not how I dressed," as an impassioned anti-rapist protest and reminder of the importance of female lives.[1]

As the dancers revealed on the dance floor, as the singers remind us, women do not live to be targeted, criticized, erased, scorned, abused, raped, or murdered. The indignities women suffer are the faults of individual participants in cultures that minimize and deride females, and in no ways the faults of girls and women themselves.

When the Michoacán women danced, they made a series of statements. These statements included the fact that females and their decisions about their lives mattered. That women and girls lived in time to be seen, heard, felt, and appreciated. That women's lives in time frequently have been compendiums of an array of temporal choices and decisions. That female presence was and remains a complex one, worthy of dignity and respect. That when girls' and women's voices differ from those of others, they deserve to be heard. That is to say, unlike Paz and an array of writers, thinkers, and historians who at times seem to have assumed worlds without female presence, unlike the murderers and rapists who treat females as objects deserving annihilation, the Michoacán girls and women demonstrated the significance of courageous female presences in time and space. Their dance was, after all, a dance in which they embodied revolutionary freedom.[2]

Despite Paz's persistent sway within the realm of Mexican poetics and also within the realms of gendered and cultural history, because of the importance of the dancers' approaches to feminine freedom, because of the depth of courage and range their physical languages suggest, it may be worth pondering, even expanding on their conversation with Paz. That is, how do significant Mexican artists focusing on gender communicate with what I see as the dancers' clamors for gendered liberty? What sort of female experiences in modern Mexico did the acclaimed Mexican poet and novelist Rosario Castellanos depict? How did the filmmaker Alfonso Cuarón communicate the voice and agency of the servant Cleo in his film *Roma*? And what, too, of contemporary Mexican and international voices raised in song against Mexican and Latin American femicide?

In most of these cases, Mexico's history of capitalism and patriarchy, its longstanding use of females within contexts of gendered inequality, has meant that artists and activists have depicted—or used—an array of gendered voices. If at times these voices have been constrained, at times harsh, at other times they have defied gendered constraints. In still other cases, female voices have shared the open, celebratory approaches the Michoacán dancers created. What, then, do these artists and activists say?

In the case of Rosario Castellanos's title character Modesta Gómez, it is worth considering how Modesta Gómez's decisions—expressed through language and behavior—communicated Castellanos's perspective on the ways capitalist patriarchy at least partially defined and harmed twentieth-century Mexican states like Chiapas, the fictional birthplace of Modesta Gómez.[3]

There, early in her life, Modesta Gómez learned that her family found itself so impoverished they couldn't afford to support her. Instead, they forced her into domestic servitude for the Ochoa family.[4] Though initially enthralled that her new living circumstances were within a home boasting luxurious furnishings, Modesta Gómez soon learned that the terms of her job included serving Jorgito, a boy just her age with whom she became inseparable. The disparities in their social positions became evident when Jorgito was sent to school and Modesta Gómez found herself forced to find wood to feed the fire, draw well water, and tend the pigs.[5]

The disparities intensified when Jorgito burst into Modesta Gómez's room one night. There, as though Modesta only existed to enable Jorgito to mis-treat her in any fashion he wished, he initiated a pattern of repeated sexual abuse, a pattern based on the cultural assumptions that impoverished Mexican girls and women lacked all rights, including the rights to self-protection. That is, Jorgito participated in a longstanding pattern of gendered mistreatment in which wealthy families have utilized impoverished women to endure their sons' sexual abuse.

Learning that her son had raped and impregnated Modesta, Jorgito's mother attempted to erase all familial involvement in that rape by blaming Modesta. As she told her, "You ungrateful little slut. And what did you think would happen? That I was going to cover up for your carrying on? Not on your life. I have a husband that I have to answer to, daughters that I need to have good examples for. So I want you out of here right now."[6]

How, then, did Modesta respond to her situation? Through linguistic strategies of inner rumination, flashforwards, and flashbacks, Castellanos invited readers inside the worlds of Modesta Gómez's sensibility. Crucially, Castellanos devised a sensibility based on the patriarchal world in which female experiences and expression were severely limited, and in which the central behavior models were brutal ones. For instance, while musing on and dreaming about her life, Modesta considered the sorts of occupations, the kinds of public and private roles she sought. These included "being the lawfully married wife of an artisan," working as a prostitute, or becoming the mistress of a wealthy man who also enabled her to set up her own business.[7]

In this world in which even the smallest female desire for happiness or appreciation was likely to be denied, Modesta Gómez's aspirations for a man able to treat her with appreciation and kindness were undermined by the arrogance and brutality of the man she married, Alberto Gómez. A person who drank profusely and beat her repeatedly, Modesta's husband also com-municated to her that he had done her a favor to marry her and that she deserved the violent abuse she received from him. Remembering that abuse but also revealing the context filled with demands that females be grateful for male involvement with them, no matter how sadistic, Modesta thought "Alberto had come through for Modesta at just the right time, when everyone had turned their backs on her so as not to see her dishonor."[8]

Further, as though she viewed her only chance of happiness could emerge by mistreating people she viewed as even less socially important than she,

Modesta Gómez took on the job of "ambusher." That work required her to wander the streets seeking out Indigenous traders, attack them, physically brutalize them, and steal their possessions.[9] Rather than emerging with empathy or even sympathy for the Indigenous people she attacked, Modesta revealed that she enjoyed mistreating Indigenous people through ambushing them. Describing her assessment of the job, Castellanos depicted Modesta Gómez's responses to ambushing: "It was true what they said. An ambusher's job was hard, and there's not much profit in it. She looked at her bloody fingernails. She didn't know why, but she was content."[10]

By granting Modesta Gómez such a disappointed and self-deriding sensibility, by also enabling her not only to behave cruelly toward Indigenous women, Castellanos suggests some of the personal repercussions emerging from Mexico's longstanding and persistent institutional and personal decisions to mistreat females. That is, Castellanos encased Modesta Gómez's experiences and her comments about those experiences, within a seemingly endless time-scape, one in which dignity and freedom for impoverished and/ or Indigenous Mexican girls and women hardly existed.

What, though, of Alfonso Cuarón's focus on modern Mexican gender relations in his internationally acclaimed movie *Roma?*[11] Whose voices in time matter, and how? What do Mexican female voices, voices consistently constrained by class and ethnicity, say? In *Roma*, Cuarón suggests that Cleo, the bilingual female servant working for a Mexico City middle-class family in the 1970s, initially spoke eloquently for others. He further suggests that much of her communication emerged through the array of tasks she was paid to perform, tasks I see as demanding that she undermine her own personality in the interest of tending to the needs of the parents, grandmother, and four children in a family soon to be altered by divorce.

While Cleo's workload as proto-parent for the children predominates, the emphasis both on her deep capacities to care for other people's children and her apparent self-abnegation speaks about the widespread refusal to alter harsh, structural gendered institutions and circumstances. Indeed, Cleo's generous and affectional approach to the children for whom she cares provides a striking contrast to the limitations placed on her personal choices.

Unlike Castellanos's portrayal of Modesta Gómez's intensifying cruelty, Cuarón portrays Cleo as a nearly entirely selfless, deeply quiet servant, particularly when she is depicted in relationship with individuals possessing power over her. One example emerged in the depictions of Cleo's relationship with her lover Fermín, a man Cleo initially found seductive and engaging but who emerged as dishonest and cruel. Indeed, after impregnating Cleo, Fermín abandons her. When Cleo seeks him out, he denies paternity, verbally abuses Cleo, and attempts to shame her.

How did this emotional abandonment of Cleo and the child-to-be affect her voice? By portraying Cleo's pregnancy as one in which she continued to work as a servant with no help from Fermín, by portraying Cleo's central conversations as those she had with children and with other women, Cuarón depicts a world of unjust gendered isolation. Abandoned by Fermín, Cleo carries the fetus, then risks her life to bear her and Fermín's child, who is born dead. Upon returning to work, Cleo initially says almost nothing, including when the family invites her to accompany them and to continue working for them during their beach vacation to Veracruz.

There, when the children invite her to swim with them, Cleo tells them, "I don't know how to swim."[12] Nonetheless, the children's mother Sofia leaves Cleo alone in charge of the children when two of them, Sofi and Paco, swim farther and farther into the sea. Unable to see them from the shore, Cleo follows them into the ocean, eventually discovering them underwater. Pulling them out, Cleo drags them to safety.

Once Sofia returns, the children tell her what happened and point out that Cleo saved their lives. At that point, the children and Sofia express gratitude and affection toward Cleo, prompting Cleo to reveal something she had not communicated earlier. As though her experience risking her life to save those of the children proved revelatory for her, Cleo tells them, "I didn't want her to be born."[13]

While this comment goes unmediated in the film, viewers are left to consider whether Cleo's experiences risking her life to save those of the children themselves prompted Cleo to recognize within herself the depth of her love for the children for whom she was paid to care. At the same time, her comment and its rationale may have been born of multifaceted recognitions and rationales.

That is, Cleo's comment can be understood as a recognition of the difficulties—even for a middle-class urban Mexican family—of protecting their children. It can be viewed as a condemnation of a country and a culture that failed to adequately protect women and children. It can also be understood as Cleo's view of the potential limitations surrounding her abilities to amply provide for and protect a child. Perhaps most significantly, Cleo's statement—within the context of her life-saving feats—may have revealed to her that, notwithstanding the depth of her abilities to love others, those very abilities were imperiled by the larger Mexican class-bound, racialized, gendered culture.[14]

How, then, do Mexican and Latin American women's voices respond to contemporary efforts to silence them? How do the dancers and their courage communicate with the array of women who have responded to femicide in Mexico and throughout Latin America? If the Mexican dancers spoke through the women's leagues, through burning the iconography used to demand female abnegation and silence, and, most especially, through their dance in the church, contemporary Latin American women have responded to the ideas that females exist only to serve men and boys, that any other form of female existence deserves rape, torture, mutilation, disappearance, and death, through feminist mobilization, marches, and song.[15]

Indeed, the anthem "Un Violador en tu camino" (translated as "The Rapist in Your Path") directly communicates female decisions to speak out for girls' and women's rights to live freely—their (read: our) rights to live without shame for their choices about what to do, where to go, how to communicate, how to dress, and how to be. As they sing and dance, "It wasn't my fault, not where I was, nor how I was dressed . . . the rapist is you."[16]

Just as Soledad Barragan's revelations about her, her friends, and her mother's experiences on the dance floor, her insistence that the dancers wore "ordinary workday clothes" that night suggests her view that females never deserved to be humiliated for their dress, for their complex, multifaceted language of dance, at once religious and anticlerical, at once an instant in which their bodies voiced their temporal presences and their potential futures in time, so too the women who have risen up against femicide remind listeners that as females they are not simply to be disregarded or viewed as victims of rape and murder, but instead seen and treated as individuals who continue to agitate, organize, communicate, and transform conditions in time, as women who, like the Michoacán women, dance on the sun stone.

NOTES

Introduction

1. Octavio Paz, *The Labyrinth of Solitude: Life and Thought in Mexico* (New York: Grove Press, 1961) Octavio Paz, *The Other Mexico: Critique of the Pyramid* (New York: Grove Press, 1972). The literature focusing on Paz and his poetics is understandably vast. Some of the works I found most helpful for this study include Jean Franco, *An Introduction to Spanish-American Literature* (Cambridge: Cambridge University Press, 1994); Enrique Krause, *Redeemers: Ideas and Power in Latin America* (New York: Harper Collins, 2011); Rachel Phillips, *The Poetic Modes of Octavio Paz* (Oxford: Oxford University Press, 1972); Elena Poniatowska, *Las Palabras del Arbol* (Barcelona: Plaza Janés, 1998); Ilan Stavans, *Octavio Paz: A Meditation* (Tucson: University of Arizona Press, 2001); and Jason Wilson, *Octavio Paz* (Boston: Twayne Publishers, 1986).

2. While Paz's "Sun Stone" was initially published in 1957, for this assessment I depend on Octavio Paz, *Sun Stone/Piedra de Sol*, trans. Eliot Weinberger (New York: New Directions, 1987). See also Octavio Paz, *Configurations*, which contains "Piedra de Sol/Sun Stone," trans. Muriel Rukeyser (New York: New Directions), 2–35.

3. The rationale informing this ignorance seems to be akin to that defining Paz's own approaches to women, and indeed, to time. That is, just as the female involvement with Mexican history remained ignored or misunderstood by Paz, so too did his critics refrain from linking Mexico's time-scape with Mexican females. Instead, critics frequently suggest that Paz's ability to devise a circular poetic structure suggestive of Aztec understandings of circular time left them agog. Then, too, the literary devise of creating a narrative voice placed in a poetic background populated with women (sometimes understood as various examples of the same woman) intrigued some of the critics who considered "Sun Stone" a love poem. Yet despite the insightful approaches of many of the critics, in many of their studies there persists an unstated cultural assumption shared with Paz, the subconscious bias that Mexican women and girls mattered less than boys and men, leaving the relationship between women and Mexican temporal history—the very history Paz sought to re-create, the very history that entrapped his speaker—invisible. For exceptions,

see Claudio Lomnitz's insightful recent assessment of Paz's cultural studies, "El ensayista en su centenario," *Nexos*, January 1, 2014, and Sandra Cypress, *Uncivil Wars: Elena Garro, Octavio Paz and the Battle for Cultural Memory: From History to Myth* (Austin: University of Texas Press, 1991).

4. Though when I began my journey as a scholar of the history of Mexican gender relations, much about the remarkable expanse of female experiences remained unstudied, at this point an array of exceptional works reveals both the significance of women and crucial ways to theorize women's Latin American lives and experiences. See in particular Silvia Arrom, *The Women of Mexico City, 1790–1857* (Stanford: Stanford University Press, 1985); Ruth Behar, *Translated Woman: Crossing the Border with Esperanza's Story* (Boston: Beacon Press, 1993); Margaret Chowning, *Rebellious Nuns: The Troubled History of a Mexican Convent, 1754–1863* (Oxford: Oxford University Press, 2006); Florencia Mallon, *Peasant and Nation: The Making of Postcolonial Mexico and Peru* (Berkeley: The University of California Press, 1995); Elena Poniatowska, *Hasta no verte Jesús mio* (Mexico City: Ediciones era, 1969); Steve J. Stern, *The Secret History of Gender: Women, Men and Power in Late Colonial Mexico* (Chapel Hill: University of North Carolina Press, 1995); Mary Kay Vaughan, *Cultural Politics in Revolution: Teachers, Peasants and the Schools in Mexico, 1930–1940* (Tucson: University of Arizona Press, 1997); Mary Kay Vaughan, Jocelyn Olcott, and Gabriela Cano, eds., *Sex in Revolution: Gender, Politics, and Power in Modern Mexico* (Durham: Duke University Press, 2006).

During the past two decades, the field of Mexican (and Latin American) women's and gendered history has expanded in important ways. See, for example, the following: William French, *The Heat in the Glass Jar: Love Letters, Bodies and the Law in Mexico* (Lincoln: University of Nebraska Press, 2015); Veronica Oikion Solano, *Cuca Garcia (1989–1973), por las causas de las mujeres y la revolución* (Zamora: El Colegio de Michoacán y El Colegio de San Luis, 2018); Jocelyn Olcott, *Revolutionary Women in Post-Revolutionary Mexico* (Durham: Duke University Press, 2006); Jocelyn Olcott, *International Women's Year: The Greatest Consciousness Raising Event in History* (New York: Oxford University Press, 2017); Susie Porter, *From Angel to Office Worker: Middle-Class Identity and Female Consciousness in Mexico, 1890–1950* (Lincoln: University of Nebraska Press, 1918); Susie Porter, *Working Women in Mexico City: Public Discourses and Material Conditions, 1979–1931*) (Tucson: University of Arizona Press, 2003); Heather Fowler Salamini and Mary Kay Vaughan, eds., *Women of the Mexican Countryside, 1830–1990* (Tucson: University of Arizona Press, 1994); Florencia Mallon, "Exploring the Origins of Democratic Patriarchy in Mexico: Gender and Popular Resistance in Puebla Highlands, 1850–1876," in *Women of the Mexican Countryside*, 3–26, eds. Fowler-Salamini and Vaughan; Deborah Cohen, Anne Rubenstein, and Victor M. Gonzalez (eds.), *Mas-*

culinity and Sexuality in Modern Mexico (Albuquerque: University of New Mexico Press, 2012); Kristina Boylan, "Gendering the Faith and Altering the Nation: The Union Femenína Católica Mexicana and Women's Revolutionary Experiences (1917–1940)," in Gabriela Cano, Jocelyn Olcott, and Mary Kay Vaughan, Gender, Politics, and Power in Modern Mexico (Durham: Duke University Press, 2006); Lessie Jo Frazier, Desired States: Sex, Gender, and Political Culture in Chile (New Brunswick: Rutgers University Press, 2020); Milada Bazant, Laura Mendez de Cuenca, Mexican Feminist, 1853–1928 (Tucson: University of Arizona Press, 2018); Nicole Sanders, Gender and Welfare in Mexico: The Consolidation of a Postrevolutionary State (University Park: Penn State University Press, 2011); Veronica Oikion, "Cuca Garcia: trazando el surco socialista a través de la Educación," Signos Históricos 17, no. 34 (Mexico, Jul/dic. 2015); Mary Kay Vaughan, "Modernizing Patriarchy: State policies, Rural Households and Women in Mexico, 1934–1940," in Elizabeth Dore and Maxine Molyneux, eds., Hidden Histories of Gender and the State in Latin America (Durham: Duke University Press, 2006); Maria Teresa Fernandez, "Advocate or Cacica? Guadalupe Urza Flores: Modernizer and Peasant Political Leader in Jalisco," in Paul Gillingham and Benjamin Smith, ed., Dictablanda: Politics, Work. and Culture in Mexico, 1938–1968 (Durham: Duke University Press, 2014); Adriana Zavala, Becoming Modern, Becoming Tradition: Women, Gender, and Representation in Mexican Art (University Park: Penn State University Press, 2011); Heather Fowler Salamini, Working Women, Entrepreneurs, and the Mexican Revolution: The Coffee Culture of Cordoba, Veracruz (Lincoln: University of Nebraska Press, 2020); Silvia Arrom, Containing the Poor: The Mexico City Poorhouse, 1774–1871 (Durham: Duke University Press); Silvia Arrom, La Guerra Rodríguez: The Life and Legends of a Mexican Independence Heroine (Berkeley: University of California Press, 2021); and many more.

5. I was fortunate enough to present parts of this chapter to the English Department at the University of Southern California as "Dancing on the Sun Stone: When Mexican Women Consider Paz" on March 23, 2015. I am particularly grateful to the English Department, and most particularly, to David St. John, for their helpful responses to my work.

6. Katharine Du Pre Lumpkin, The Making of a Southerner (Westport, CT: Greenwood Press, 1971) prompted my interest in Lumpkin's remarkable approach to the politics of southern family relations. I interviewed her in Charlottesville, Virginia, in 1974 in order to complete my honors essay, "Lumpkin's South."

7. And abilities. Yes, I got jobs working at McDonalds, and yes, I worked as a domestic for the belly dancer and for several university professors. My competence? A sadly different story.

8. While nearly all Paraguayans speak Guaraní, an unwritten Indigenous language, in General Aquino only the handful of wealthy villagers spoke Spanish.

9. In those days, I consistently traveled with a typewriter. I also took 100 books with me to Paraguay.

10. Larry Goodwyn trained and advised many students about southern history, enabling them to focus on individuals and experiences often left out—or ill-considered—in historical studies. Certainly, that was the attitude informing the undergraduate and graduate classes I took from him. It is impossible to overstate the fashions in which he attempted to create a different, more just world.

11. This was not a passive concern; rather, I developed a research project entitled "The Mexican Women's Revolution" and sought primary sources to inform that project in the university archives at Harvard, Yale, Princeton, and Rutgers.

12. See Marjorie Becker, "Lázaro Cárdenas and the Mexican Counter-Revolution: The Struggle over Culture in Michoacán, 1934–1940," doctoral dissertation, Yale University, 1988.

13. Interview with Carlos Martínez, Ario de Rayon, Michoacán, September, 1985.

14. The literature focusing on Cárdenas was quite intriguing and expansive when I initially entered this intellectual arena. For my assessment of it from a grassroots democratic perspective, see Marjorie Becker, *Setting the Virgin on Fire: Lázaro Cárdenas, Michoacán Peasants, and the Redemption of the* Mexican Revolution (Berkeley: University of California Press, 1995), 1–9. I was fortunate enough to meet Vaughan in the SEP archives in Mexico City where each of us was conducting research; my conversations with her then and over the years have proved deeply enlightening. Her approach to the Cardenista education program remains crucial in her *Cultural Politics*. See also Alan Knight's important article, "Cardenismo: Juggernaut or Jalopy," *Journal of Latin American Studies* 26, no. 1 (Feb. 2004), 73–107.

15. Emilia da Costa reminded me that C. Vann Woodward used this approach; certainly, I have long revered Woodward's works about the US South and could only hope that I could somehow employ his strategy effectively.

16. I remain grateful to the editors at the University of California Press, which published *Setting the Virgin on Fire*.

17. Gilbert M. Joseph and Daniel Nugent, eds., *Everyday Forms of State Formation: Revolution and the Negotiation of Rule in Modern Mexico* (Durham: Duke University Press, 1994). See in particular James C. Scott, foreword to *Everyday Forms*, ed. Joseph and Nugent, xi–xii, and Florencia Mallon, "Reflection on the Ruins: Everyday Forms of State Formation in Nineteenth Century Mexico," in *Everyday Forms*, 69–106.

18. I discuss this perspective that I developed in some detail in *Setting the Virgin on Fire*, 7–8.

19. Marjorie Becker, "Torching La Purísima, Dancing at the Altar: The Con-

struction of Revolutionary Hegemony in Michoacán, 1934–1940," in Joseph and Nugent, eds., *Everyday Forms*, 247–64.

20. Becker, "Torching La Purísima," 252–53.

21. The initial conference focusing on what came to be known as "innovative historical writing" was entitled "Narrating Histories" and was held at the California Institute of Technology, April 1–2, 1994. The conference led to the development of the international journal, *Rethinking History: The Journal of Theory and Practice*.

22. See in particular Hayden White's innovative *Metahistory: The Historical Imagination in Nineteenth-Century Europe* (Baltimore: The Johns Hopkins University Press, 1973), informed by his brilliant insights about the poetics' defining conventional historical writing. See also Robert Rosenstone, *The Mirror in the Shrine: American Encounters with Meiji Japan* (Cambridge: Harvard University Press, 1988) and James Goodman, *But Where is the Lamb: Imagining the Story of Abraham and Isaac* (New York: Schocken Books, 2013).

23. For a recent Latin Americanist example of innovative historical writing, see Ezer Vierba, *The Singer's Needle: An Undisciplined History of Panamá* (Chicago: University of Chicago Press, 2021).

24. Becker, "Torching la Purísima, Dancing at the Altar."

25. Marjorie Becker, "When I Was a Child, I Danced as a Child, but Now That I Am Old, I Think About Salvation: Concepción González and a Past That Would Not Stay Put," *Rethinking History: The Journal of Theory and Practice* 1, no. 3 (Winter 1997), 343–55.

26. Marjorie Becker, "As Though They Meant Her No Harm, María Enríquez Remade the Friends Who Abandoned Her—Their Intentions, Their Possibilities, Their Worlds—Inviting Them (Perhaps, It Is True) to Dance," *Rethinking History: The Journal of Theory and Practice* 12, no. 2 (June 2008), 153–64.

27. Becker, "As Though They Meant Her No Harm," 154.

28. Fernando Foglio Miramontes, *Geografía económica agrícola del estado de Michoacán*, 4 vols., (Mexico DR: Editorial Cultura, 1936), most especially 2:168. A series of interviews focusing on work habits; spiritual, social, political, and economic life; possessions; and use of time reveal a compelling portrait of the Michoacán gendered time-scape. Interviews with Maria Elena Verduzco de Peña, Ario de Rayón, April—July and November, 1990; Esperanza Rocha, Ario de Rayón, May 13 and June 2, 1990; Concepción Méndez, Ario de Rayón, June 9 and November 3, 1990; Rafael Ochoa, Ario de Rayón, May—June, November, 1990.

29. Precisely because Mexican women experienced such persistent unappreciated workloads in time, their temporal experiences became "ghostly," as I attempt to show in "As Though They Meant Her No Harm," 157–58.

30. For more on sexual assault against Mexican and other Latin American women, see Becker, "As Though They Meant Her No Harm."

31. Marjorie Becker, "Talking Back to Frida: Houses of Emotional Mestizaje," *History and Theory*, *Theme Issue* 41 (December 2002), 56–71. This article was re-published by *History and Theory* in the volume *Theorizing Race, Past and Present*, February 2021.

32. Series of interviews with Carrie Popper Becker, Peggy Popper, Mary Rainey, and Marvin Jerome Becker focusing on Black and Jewish experiences of Macon's racialized Bible Belt context, conducted in Macon, Georgia from 1972 to 2000.

33. Becker, "Talking Back to Frida," 69–70.

34. Becker, "Talking Back to Frida," 71.

35. The fact that I myself was repeatedly sexually assaulted in rural Michoacán prompted me extensively to alter my career path. As sometimes happens to sexual assault victims and survivors, this prompted a painful invisibility. I assess this issue, and its personal and professional consequences, in my "You Grabbed Me as Though You Owned My Body, But I'm Here to Say You're Wrong: Toward a Letter to the Zamora Sexual Assailant," *Rethinking History: A Journal of Theory and Practice* 25, no. 1 (2021), 11–20.

36. See Hans Kellner's *Language and Historical Representation: Getting the Story Crooked* (Madison: The University of Wisconsin Press, 1989) for an insightful approach to some of the historical and literary challenges I have explored. And for renditions of the sort of complex, multi-voiced, and multifaceted approaches to history that deeply encouraged me, see Rosenstone, *Mirror in the Shrine*; Robert Rosenstone, *The Man Who Swam into History: The (Mostly) True Story of My Jewish Family* (Austin: The University of Texas Press, 2005); and Goodman, *But Where Is the Lamb*. For a compelling approach to historical and literary engagement, see Rosa Isolde Reuque Paillalef, *When a Flower Is Reborn: The Life and Times of a Mapuche Feminist*, ed. and trans. Florencia Mallon (Durham: Duke University Press, 2002).

37. Marjorie Becker, *Body Bach* (Huntington Beach, CA: Tebot Bach, 2005); Marjorie Becker, *Glass Piano/Piano Glass* (Huntington Beach: Tebot Bach, 2010; Marjorie Becker, *The Macon Sex School: Songs of Tenderness and Resistance* (Tebot Bach, 2020).

38. "Oral Poetry," in Alex Preminger and T.V. F. Brogan, eds., *The New Princeton Encyclopedia of Poetry and Poetics* (Princeton: Princeton University Press, 1993), 862–66. See also Donald Hall, *Goatfoot Milktongue Twinbird: Interviews, Essays and Notes on Poetry, 1970–76* (Ann Arbor: The University of Michigan Press, 1978).

39. See my article, "Music, Such Sudden Music: When Mexican Women Altered Space in Time," *Rethinking History: The Journal of History and Practice* 23, no. 1 (2019), 2–15. I presented this historical fable at the Stanford University History Department symposium, "Violence and Its Definitions in Modern Latin America,"

in March 2017. I also presented it at the celebration of the careers of Florencia Mallon and Steve J. Stern, a conference entitled "Researching, Reading, and Writing Latin American History: Theory, Method Politics," January 3–4, 2018, at the University of Maryland Mexican Cultural Institute.

Chapter One

1. Despite the now extensive historical literature focusing on Latin American and Mexican women, it was Paz's critical and poetic work and my historical training that alerted me to ways that scholars and historians have understood time itself as a background upon which men and boys, but seldom girls and women behave. It was these reflections that generated my understanding of time and of voice as gendered. For a trailblazing study revealing multiple instances of male mistreatment of women within Latin America's capitalist context, a study that also reveals complex examples of female resistance and the complicated use of gendered stereotypes, see Steve J. Stern, *The Secret History of Gender: Women, Men and Power in Late Colonial Mexico* (Chapel Hill: University of North Carolina Press, 1995).

2. For an important study focusing on colonial Michoacán, see Jim Krippner Martínez, *Rereading the Conquest: The History of Early Colonial Michoacán, 1521–1565* (University Park: Pennsylvania University Press, 2001).

3. Jean Meyer's crucial three-volume study of the Cristero rebellion remains the critical work for those seeking to understand this important church-state civil war, most especially the grassroots counterrevolutionary rationales prompting so many men in western Mexico to rise up against the revolutionary government. See Jean Meyer, *La Cristiada*, trans. Aurelio Garzón del Camino. 2nd ed. 3 vols. (Mexico City: Siglo XXI Editores, 1974). See also Jean Meyer, "An Idea of Mexico: Catholics in the Revolution," in *The Eagle and the Virgin: Nation and Cultural Revolution in Mexico, 1920–1940*, eds. Mary Kay Vaughan and Stephen E. Lewis (Durham: Duke University Press, 2006), 281–96.

4. Ethnohistorical methods proved crucial to the development of a modern Mexican cultural history sensitive to peasant complexity. Remarkable examples of these methods include Paul Friedrich, *The Princes of Naranja: An Essay in Ethnohistorical Method* (Austin: University of Texas Press, 1989); and James C. Scott, foreword to Gilbert M. Joseph and Daniel Nugent, *Everyday Forms of State Formation: Revolution and Negotiation of Rule in Modern Mexico* (Durham: Duke University Press, 1994), vii–xii. See also James C. Scott, *The Weapons of the Weak: Everyday Forms of Peasant Resistance* (New Haven: Yale University Press, 1985). I am deeply grateful to Jim Scott for many conversations regarding peasant culture and for his invitation to participate in what he referred to as "the Yale School of the Peasantry," to Paul Friedrich for our conversation about Michoacán's development

of rural bossism, to Luis González y González and Armida de la Vara for a long-standing dialogue about Michoacán political culture, and to Mary Kay Vaughan for her early attention to my efforts to recognize the complexity and nascent democratic gestures of Mexican women and men.

5. As I will discuss below, the Tarascan woman painting the pearls worked for Mari Elena Verduzco de Peña. Verduzco de Peña possessed a copious memory about northwestern Michoacán history and social relations as my multiple interviews with her revealed. As I will discuss, at times she conducted her dressmaking business during the interviews. Interviews with Mari Elena Verduzco de Peña, Ario de Rayon, Michoacán, April, May, July, and November 1990.

6. Mexican miscegenation between Spaniards and Indigenous women emerged in the sixteenth century. The connections between Mexico's Indigenous natives, Spaniards, and imported African enslaved people created national and Michoacán populations numerically dominated by mestizas/os. Still, when I first conducted research about this topic, historiographic assessments were limited. Thus, I spent considerable time developing an assessment of Mexico and Michoacán populations based on a diverse array of categories focusing on ethnicity, religion, political affiliation, class, and, most particularly, gender. See Marjorie Becker, *Setting the Virgin on Fire: Lázaro Cárdenas, Michoacán Peasants, and the Redemption of the Mexican Revolution* (Berkeley: University of California Press, 2006), 8, 35, 38–39. Crucial subsequent assessments focusing on Mexican racial and ethnic histories include Alexander Dawson, *Indian and Nation in Revolutionary Mexico* (Tucson: University of Arizona Press, 2004) and Maria Elena Martinez, *Genealogical Fictions: Limpieza de Sangre, Religion, and Gender in Colonial Mexico* (Stanford: Stanford University Press, 2008). I remain deeply grateful to Arnulfo Embriz Osorio for introducing me to landmarks of Morelia architecture and for our extensive dialogue about Michoacán revolutionary and counterrevolutionary peasants.

7. See Becker, "As though they meant her no harm."

8. While few scholars focus on female temporality and none I know of have considered Michoacán female time-scapes in relationship to Paz's perspectives on time, the exceptionally intriguing scholarship on gender relations in Latin America has deeply altered the scholarly landscape. Certainly, Steve Stern's assessment of the fact that many Mexican women found themselves compelled to spend up to three women-hours a day making tortillas has revealed key historical aspects of Mexican female experiences of time. For another approach to Mexican women's involvement with tortilla-making, see Oscar Lewis, *Five Families: Mexican Case Studies in the Culture of Poverty* (New York: Basic Books, 1975), 25. Of particular interest remains Heather Fowler-Salamini and Mary Kay Vaughan's *Women in the Mexican Countryside, 1850–1990: Creating Spaces, Shaping Transition*. In that volume, see in particular Maria da Gloria Marroni de Velázuez, "Changes in Rural Society and

Domestic Labor in Atlizco Puebla, 1940–1990," and Gail Mummert, "From Metate to Despate: Rural Women's Salaries Labor and the Redefinition of Gendered Spaces and Roles."

9. Interviews with Rafael Ochoa González, Ario de Rayón, Michoacán, May, June, and November 1990; interviews with Verduzco de Peña, April 1990.

10. Interview with Ochoa González, May 1990.

11. For population figures, see Fernando Foglio Miramontes, *Geografía económica agrícola del estado de Michoacán* (Mexico City: Editorial Cultural, 1936).

12. See Luis González y González, *San José de Gracia: Mexican Village in Transition*, trans. John Upton (Austin: University of Texas Press, 1972); and Griselda Villegas Muñoz, *Emilia, Una Mujer de Jiquilpan* (Jiquilpan de Juarez: Centro de Estudios de la Revolución Mexicana Lázaro Cárdenas, A.C., 1984).

13. Octavio Paz, *Sunstone/Piedra de Sol*, trans. Eliot Weinberger (New York: New Directions, 1987).

14. Interview with José Corona Nuñez, Morelia, Michoacán, July 11, 1989. Corona Nuñez's perspective on female housework was shared by Jesus Múgica Martínez in interviews in Morelia, Michoacán, December 4, 1984; July 11, 1988; July 10, 1989; August 3, 1989; and with Hilario Reyes Garibaldi in interviews conducted in Morelia, Michoacán, on July 18 1985, and June 26, 1990. Interview with Luis Amezcua, Ario de Rayón, May 28, 1990.

15. Interviews with Jesus Múgica Martínez, Morelia, Michoacán, December 4, 1984; July 11, 1988; July 10, 1989; August 3. 1989; interviews with Hilario Reyes Garibaldi, Morelia Michoacán, July 18, 1985, and June 26, 1990.

16. Interview with Concepción Méndez, Ario de Rayón, Michoacán, November 1990.

17. Interview with Concepción Méndez, Ario de Rayón, Michoacán, November 1990.

18. Interview with Concepción Méndez, Ario de Rayón, Michoacán, November 1990.

19. For thoughtful studies discussing historical implications of this gendered division of labor in colonial and modern Latin America, see Arnold Bauer, *Goods, Power, and History: Latin America's Material Culture* (Cambridge, MA: Cambridge University Press, 2010); Steve J. Stern, *The Secret History of Gender: Women, Men, and Power in Late Colonial Mexico* (Chapel Hill: University of North Carolina Press, 1995); Jeffrey M. Pilcher, *¡Que vivan los tamales!* (Albuquerque: University of New Mexico Press, 1998); and Guillermo Bonfil Batalla, *México Profundo: Una civilización negada* (Mexico City: Editorial Grijalbo, 1987). See also María da Gloria Marroni Velázquez, "Changes in Domestic Labor in Atlixco, Puebla, 1940–1990," in *Women of the Mexican Countryside: Creating Spaces, Shaping Transitions*, Heather Fowler-Salamini and Mary Kay Vaughan, eds. (Tucson: University of Arizona Press, 1994.)

20. For an important comparison of the temporal geography characteristic of colonial Mexican and colonial Andean women's food-defined workloads, see Bauer, *Goods, Power, and History*, 28–30.

21. These specific descriptive details emerged through an array of interviews about northwestern Michoacán's material culture. They include my interview with Méndez, November 1990; an interview with Verduzco de Peña, July 1990; interviews with Ignacio Espitia, Zamora, Michoacán, August 18, 1985, and August 25, 1985; and interviews with Corona Nuñez, July 11, 1989.

22. On the cultural significance of appearance, interviews with Soledad Barragan, Ario de Rayón, Michoacán, June 1990, and with Francisco Elizalde, Zamora, Michoacán, June 1988.

23. A series of Michoacán weavings I collected depict laundry women—no laundry men—washing clothing at nearby streams. The weavings themselves seemed simultaneously to celebrate and perhaps to exoticize female temporal labor.

24. Sermons referring to ideal female behavior were found in the Archivo de la Purísima Corazón (APC) in Zamora, Michoacán. For an example of the material priests used to craft sermons, see "Acta de consegración a la Santísima Virgin de Guadalupe," Othon Nuñez de Zarate, circular 52, November 20, 1921), caja 13, Sacramental y Disciplina, 1902–1930. In addition, my interviews with Verduzco de Peña in Ario de Rayón, April and May 1990; with Esperanza Rocha in Ario de Rayón, June 2, 1990; and with Carmen Valadez de García in Ario de Rayón, June 1990, revealed much about the gendered religious culture.

25. An array of northwestern Michoacán women and men emerged as individuals possessing keen memories about extensive bodies of information. They included Rocha, Verduzco de Peña, and Concepción Méndez whom I interviewed in Ario de Rayón in June and November 1990. The same should be said about Ignacio Espitia, whom I interviewed in Zamora in August 1985; and Ochoa González, who I interviewed in May, July, and November 1990.

26. "Instruido en contra de Antonio Mendoza por el crimen de rapto, August 13, 1924, Expediente 13-923/28 ramo penales, Zamora. Juzgado de primer instancia, Estado de Michoacán, Archivo Judicial del Estado de Michoacán (AJEM).

27. Interview with Ochoa González, Ario de Rayón, November 1990. My interview with Soledad Barragán in Ario de Rayón on June 6, 1990, provided important information about her mother, Carmen Barragán, whom her daughter described as possessing a keen sense of social justice.

28. Ochoa González described the gendered journeys of Ario emigrants to Chicago in detail in his November 1990 interview with me. See also Ana Raquel Miniam, *Undocumented Lives: The Untold Story of Mexican Migration* (Cambridge, MA: Harvard University Press, 2018).

29. According to Zamora native Francisco Elizalde, Rodríguez Carbajal con-

sistently dressed in tasteful and showy ways. Rodríguez Carbajal was Zamora teacher Angelina Acosta's school inspector. In Acosta's opinion, Rodríguez Carbajal expressed herself rather dramatically because "she enjoyed doing so." Interview with Acosta, Zamora, Michoacán, November 8, 1990.

30. "Año 1925 Michoacán/Asuntos esclolares del estado," Expediente G, 12-3-9-64. Archivo Histórico de la Secretaria de Educación Pública, Mexico City (AHSEP).

31. Interview with Acosta.

32. Interview with Acosta.

33. As Acosta pointed out, though rural teachers received some educational materials from their national supervisors, it was up to teachers like her to observe students' requirements and to fashion helpful information from the materials they received.

34. Priests based their messages against the land reform and the governmental schooling on Catholic notions regarding the sanctity of private property and a belief that revolutionary teachers would draw students away from Catholic understandings of the workings of the world. To communicate these ideas to parishioners, priests could draw on approaches found in an array of Catholic prescriptive writings, such as "Normas del Comité Ejecutivo Episcopal a los Sacerdotes de los Católicos," caja 13, Sacramental y Disciplina, 1901–1940," APC.

35. While many Mexican historical documents can no longer be found because of fire, floods, war, and theft, in the process of conducting research in Michoacán I discovered that some documents have been housed in private collections. I was fortunate enough to discover many of Juan Gutiérrez's historical documents revealing aspects of his experiences serving as a local Michoacán political leader and land-reform agent in the Zamora home of his nephew. Gutiérrez's relatives kindly allowed me to assess some of the documents housed there. Other documents focusing on Gutiérrez are housed in the Archivo Municipal de Zamora (AMZ). For information regarding the women's league, see "Juan Gutiérrez to Zamora municipal president," July 15, 1936, expediente 4, 1936, Fondo Gobernación, AMZ.

36. Esperanza Rocha, Concha Méndez, and Rafael Ochoa González all maintained that many Ario villagers found participation in the women's league to be transgressive. Rocha herself, a member of the league because her husband had accepted land from the revolutionary government, suggested that the meetings were informed by passionately held views about female behavior. Interviews with Rocha, June 2, 1990; with Méndez, November 3, 1990; and with Ochoa González, May 12, 1990.

37. Matilde Anguiano to Juan Gutiérrez, July 6, 1937, loose documents, AMZ; María Loreto Pacheco to Zamora municipal president, October 19, 1937, loose documents, AMZ.

38. Matilde Anguiano to Ing. Gustavo Martínez Baca, August 9, 1937, loose documents, AMZ.

39. Interview with Carlos Martínez, Ario de Rayón, September 7, 1985; interview with Méndez, June 9, 1990; interview with Ochoa González, May 12, 1990.

40. Interview with Méndez, June 9, 1990.

41. Ibid. While Méndez described the dancers in some detail, it was Soledad Barragán, one of the dancers, whose recollections provided a crucial sense of what happened at the torching and later at the dance. Interview with Méndez, November 3, 1990, interview with Barragán.

42. Interview with Méndez.

43. Rocha suggested that numerous women and men were involved in the torching and the dance. Interview with Rocha, May 13, 1990.

44. Interview with Rocha, June 2, 1990. While *Setting the Virgin on Fire* is a cultural history focusing on, among other things, the Catholic religious world of northwestern Michoacán during the modern period, to reconsider that culture in temporal terms prompts a recognition of the multifaceted roles time played in the northwestern Michoacán Catholic imaginary. For an assessment of routine clerical approaches to parishioners, see Becker, *Setting the Virgin on Fire*, 15–16.

45. On Mexican musicians performing secular dance music, participant observation in Zamora, Michoacán, 1990. On Michoacán musicians performing traditional dance music, participant observation in Morelia, Michoacán, 1990. See, too, Charles V. Heath, *The Inevitable Bandstand: The State Band of Oaxaca and the Politics of Sound* (Lincoln: University of Nebraska Press) 2015.

Chapter Two

1. My own translation of the poem and the compelling translations of Muriel Rukeyser and Eliot Weinberger proved crucial in making "Sun Stone" part of the primary documentation for this book. See Octavio Paz, *Sun Stone/Piedra de Sol*, trans. Eliot Weinberger (New York: New Directions, 1987, 1991); Octavio Paz, "Sun Stone," in *Configurations*, trans. Muriel Rukeyser (New York: New Directions, 1965). My references are to Weinberger's translation.

2. The historical focus on the Aztecs—the Mexica, as they understood themselves—and that focusing on their post-contact descendants is now deservedly vast. Crucial works include Inga Clendinnen, *Aztecs: an Interpretation* (Cambridge, UK: Cambridge University Press, 1991); Charles Gibson, *The Aztecs under Spanish Rule: A History of the Indians in the Valley of Mexico, 1519–1810* (Stanford: Stanford University Press, 1964); Rebecca Horn, *Preconquest Coyoacan: Nahua-Spanish Relations in Central Mexico, 1529–1650* (Stanford: Stanford University Press, 1997);

James Lockhart, *The Nahuas after the Conquest: A Social and Cultural History of the Indians of Central Mexico, Sixteenth through Eighteenth Centuries* (Stanford: Stanford University Press, 1992); Jacques Soustelle, *Daily Life of the Aztecs on the Eve of the Spanish Conquest*, trans. Patrick O'Brian (Stanford: Stanford University Press, 1970). For assessments of ancient Aztec and Mayans' understanding of temporal movement as circular, see Enrique Florescano, *Memory, Myth and Time: From the Aztecs to Independence*, trans. Albert G. Bork with the assistance of Katharine R. Bork (Austin: University of Texas Press, 1994).

3. Paz, *Sunstone/Piedra de Sol*.

4. Paz, stanza 1, line 3.

5. Paz, stanza 1, lines 4–6.

6. Paz, stanza 2, line 1.

7. Paz, stanza 2, lines 1–3.

8. Paz, stanza 2, line 4.

9. Soustelle understood Aztec thought as dualistic, a view that may have influenced Paz's thinking. See Soustelle, *Daily Life of the Aztecs*.

10. Paz, *Sunstone/Piedra de Sol*, stanza 3, lines 5, 8.

11. Paz, stanza 3, line 10.

12. Paz, stanza 5, line 2.

13. Paz, stanza 5, line 4.

14. Paz, stanza 7, line 1.

15. The reference reminds of the implementation of a dependent form of industrial capitalism on mainly rural Mexico in the nineteenth century, replete with government-paid surveyors who wandered rural property long worked by "ordinary" Mexicans, surveying not its value to those who lived there, working the land, but rather for the surveyors themselves who would be rewarded with the great majority of Mexican rural property. Scholarship focusing on the implications of these approaches include Friedrich Katz, "Labor Conditions on Haciendas in Porfirian Mexico: Some Trends and Tendencies," *Hispanic American Historical Review* 57 (1974): 1–47; and John Coatsworth, "Railroads, Landholding and Agrarian Protest in the Early Porfiriato," *Hispanic American Historical Review* 57 (1974): 48–71.

16. Paz, *Sunstone/Piedra de Sol*, stanza 6, line 1.

17. Paz, stanza 6, line 3.

18. Paz, stanza 6, line 4.

19. Paz, stanza 8, lines 2–3.

20. Paz, stanza 8, lines 4–5.

21. Paz, stanza 8, line 6.

22. Paz, stanza 8, line 7.

23. Paz, stanza 8, line 7.

24. The notion of "old Mexico" frequently refers to the Mexico before the nineteenth-century efforts to introduce dependent industrial capitalism and to unify Mexico's highly complex array of peoples.

25. Charles Gibson, *Tlaxcala in the Sixteenth Century* (New Haven: Yale University Press, 1952); Inga Clendinnen, "'Fierce and Unnatural Cruelty': Cortés and the Conquest of Mexico," in *The Cost of Courage in Mexico Society: Essays on Mesoamerican Society and Culture* (Cambridge: Cambridge University Press, 2010), 49–90.

26. Paz, *Sunstone/Piedra de Sol*, stanza 10, line 2; stanza 16, line 9.

27. Paz, stanza 10, line 3.

28. Paz, stanza 10, line 5

29. Paz, stanza 12, line 1.

30. Paz, stanzas 12, 13.

31. Paz, stanza 12, lines 4, 5.

32. Paz, stanza 13, line 5.

33. Rachel Phillips, *The Poetic Modes of Octavio Paz* (Oxford: Oxford University Press, 1972), 18.

34. Paz, *Sunstone/Piedra de Sol*, stanza 13, line 6.

35. Paz, stanza 13, line 6.

36. Paz, stanza 13, line 7

37. Paz, stanza 13, line 8.

38. Paz, stanza 13, lines 9, 10.

39. Paz, stanza 13, lines 12, 13.

40. Paz, stanza 16, lines 3, 4.

41. Paz, stanza 16, line 9.

42. Paz, stanza 24, lines 6–9.

43. Paz, stanza 24, lines 11, 12.

44. Paz, stanza 24, lines 14, 15.

45. Paz, stanza 24, line 29, 30.

46. Paz, stanza 24, lines 34, 35, 36, 37.

47. The historical and poetic works focusing on the Spanish Civil War are extensive. Key works include Hugh Thomas, *The Spanish Civil War* (New York: Harper and Row Publishers, 1961); Gabriel Jackson, *A Concise History of the Spanish Civil War* (London: Thames and Hudson, 1974); George Orwell, *Homage to Catalonia* (New York: Harcourt, Brace and World, 1952); Philip Levine, *The Bread of Time: Toward an Autobiography* (New York: Alfred A. Knopf, 1995); Robert Rosenstone, *Crusade of the Left: The Lincoln Brigades in the Spanish Civil War* (New York: Pegasus, 1969); Temma Kaplan, "Gender on the Barricades," *Journal of Women's History* 9, no. 3 (Autumn 1997): 177–85.

48. Paz, *Sunstone/Piedra de Sol*, stanza 25 lines 5, 6.

49. Paz, stanza 25, lines 17,

50. Paz, stanza 25, line 16, 17.

51. Paz, stanza 25, line 20.

52. Paz, stanza 25, lines 27, 28.

53. Paz, stanza 25, line 45.

54. Paz, stanza 25, line 46.

55. Paz, stanza 25, lines 37, 38.

56. Paz, stanza 26, lines 7, 8.

57. Paz, stanza 26, line 13.

58. Paz, stanza 26, line 16.

59. Paz, stanza 26, lines 19–21.

60. Paz, stanza 26, lines 23, 25.

61. Paz, stanza 26, line 26.

62. Paz, stanza 27, lines 3, 4.

63. Paz, stanza 27, lines 5, 6.

64. Paz, stanza 27, line 14.

65. On Mexican cultural approaches to death, see Claudio Lomnitz, *Death and the Idea of Mexico* (New York: Zone Books, 2005). See, too, Kristin Norget, *Days of Death, Days of Life: Ritual in the Popular Culture of Oaxaca* (New York: Columbia University Press, 2006).

66. Paz, *Sunstone/Piedra de Sol*, stanza 30, line 8.

67. Paz, stanza 30, line 12

68. Paz, stanza 30, lines 15, 16, 19.

69. Paz, stanza 30, lines 22, 23, 24.

70. Paz, stanza 30, lines 48, 49, 50.

71. Paz, stanza 29, lines 8, 15–16.

72. Paz, stanza 32, line 1.

73. Paz, stanza 32, line 17.

74. Paz, stanza 33, lines 4, 5, 8.

75. Paz, stanza 32, line 31.

76. Paz, stanza 32, line 32.

77. Paz, stanza 33, lines 14, 15, 16.

78. Paz, stanza 33, line 29.

79. This recognition seemingly emerged in isolation from contemporary Mexican or international feminist movements or perspectives.

Chapter Three

1. Octavio Paz, *Sunstone/Piedra de Sol*, trans. Eliot Weinberger (New York: New Directions Books, 1987).

2. For a classic approach to misogynist identifications of women with the natural world, see Susan Griffin, *Women and Nature: The Roaring Inside Her* (New York: Harper and Row, 1978). For a thoughtful approach to colonial Latin American concerns regarding children and their destinies, see Bianca Premo, *Children of the Father King: Youth, Authority, and Colonial Minority in Colonial Lima, 1650–1820* (Chapel Hill: University of North Carolina Press, 2005).

3. For compelling studies focusing on death in Mexico, see Claudio Lomnitz, *Death and the Idea of Mexico* (New York: Zone Books, 2005); and Kristin Norget, *Days of Death, Days of Life: Ritual in the Popular Culture of Oaxaca* (New York: Columbia University Press, 2006).

4. Notwithstanding Diego Rivera's conventional approaches to gender relations, the notion of a new Mexican man potentially emerging from the revolution of 1910 can be found in some of Rivera's murals, particularly those displayed at Mexico City's Secretariat of Public Education. For a key study of Rivera, see Patrick Marnham, *Dreaming with His Eyes Open: A Life of Diego Rivera* (New York: Alfred W. Knopf, 1998).

5. Ironically, "Sun Stone," notwithstanding its extensive exploration of heterosexual male sexuality, can be understood as reticent, even prudish, regarding female physical realms.

6. My recognition of the gendered qualities of voice itself seeks even more historico-poetic scholarship. For an intriguing approach to issues of female voice and silence in a Roman context, see Amy Richlin, *Arguments with Silence: Writing the History of Roman Women* (Ann Arbor: University of Ann Arbor Press, 2014).

7. Paz, *Sunstone/Piedra de Sol*, stanza 24, line 7.

8. Paz, stanza 24, line 7.

9. Interviews with Francisco Elizalde, Zamora, Michoacán, July 26, 1985, June 2, 1988; interviews with Concepción Méndez, Ario de Rayón, Michoacán, November 3, 1990; conversations with Luis González y González, San José de Gracia, Michoacán, June 16, 1990. For examples of the sermons northwestern Michoacán priests delivered focusing on female sexual purity as a model for all Michoacanos, see "Carta pastoral colectiva de los prelados de la provincial de Michoacán," 1920, caja 11, Archivo de la Purísima Corazón (APC), Zamora, Michoacán.

10. Interviews with Esperanza Rocha, Ario de Rayón, July 6, 1990; Maria Elena Verduzco de Peña, Ario de Rayón, April 28, 1990. María Enríquez's rapto accusation of Antonio Mendoza also revealed elements of a culture in which genders lived largely segregated lives. See "Instruida en contra de Antonio Mendoza por el delito de rapto," August 13, 1924, expediente 13-923/28, ramo penales, Zamora, Juzgado de primer instancia, Archivo Judicial del Estado de Michoacán (AJEM), Morelia, Michoacán.

11. For an insightful assessment of Mexican women's relationships to tortilla

work, see Jeffrey M. Pilcher, *Que vivan los tamales: Food and the Making of Mexican Identity* (Albuquerque: University of New Mexico Press, 1998), 106–7. See also Oscar Lewis, *Five Families: Mexican Case Studies in the Culture of Poverty* (New York: Basic Books, 1959). Interview with Carmen Valadéz de García focusing on some of the ways acts of hospitality were seen through gendered perspectives, Ario de Rayón, June 2, 1990. Conversation with Armida de la Vara focusing on various gendered customs in northwestern Michoacán, Zamora, Michoacán, June 15, 1990.

12. Based on my training and experience in developing and analyzing the histories of grassroots democratic behavior and social movements, and my experiences as a professional journalist and my academic training in oral history, I attempted to develop and utilize a democratic approach to selecting and interviewing Michoacanos. This was largely true because I understand the histories I collected as belonging not to me, but to all Michoacanos, to all Mexicans.

13. Numerous Michoacanos participated in the 1926–1929 Cristero civil war. In addition, the revolutionary schooling established during Cárdenas's 1934–1940 presidency of Mexico prompted an array of violent responses. See Marjorie Becker, *Setting the Virgin on Fire: Lázaro Cárdenas, Michoacán Peasants, and the Redemption of the Mexican Revolution* (Berkeley: University of California Press, 1996), 124–25.

14. Interviews with Verduzco de Peña, Rocha, Méndez, Valadéz de García; interview with Soledad Barragán, Ario de Rayón, June 6, 1990.

15. Many concerns regarding trust emerge in oral-history interviews conducted by outsiders. As Francisco Elizalde long ago reminded me, the necessity of developing an approach including trust and alertness to language's own plastic potential is crucial. Interview with Elizalde, Zamora, Michoacán, June 2, 1988. I also long have benefited from an extensive series of conversations with acclaimed Latin American historian and novelist Florencia Mallon regarding fashions of fairly assessing quite complex, at times impoverished individuals.

16. "Instruido en contra de Antonio Mendoza por el delito de rapto," August 13, 1924.

17. "Instruido en contra de Antonio Mendoza por el delito de rapto," August 13, 1924.

18. "Instruido en contra de Antonio Mendoza por el delito de rapto," August 13, 1924.

19. "Instruido en contra de Antonio Mendoza por el delito de rapto," August 13, 1924.

20. Interviews with José Corona Nuñez, Morelia, Michoacán, July 11, 1989; and with Verduzco de Peña, April 27, 1990. During Verduzco de Peña's childhood, she was allowed to socialize with Tarascan children.

21. Interview with Méndez.

22. Interviews with Méndez, Verduzco de Peña, and Esperanza Rocha provided crucial material enabling my understanding of the array of tasks women and at times their daughters performed. Interview with Rocha, Ario de Rayón, July 6, 1990. Soledad Barragán's assessment of the challenging life underpaid men endured on the ranchos proved evocative. Interview with Soledad Barragán, Ario de Rayón, June 6, 1990.

23. That the schools were public and coeducational presented both new opportunities and, for some, new concerns, as my interviews with Francisco Elizalde who attended one such school and Angelina Acosta who taught in another suggested. Interview with Elizalde, November 5, 1990; interview with Angelina Acosta, Zamora, Michoacán, November 8, 1990.

24. Interview with Méndez.

25. See Hans Kellner's provocative approaches to certain yet unwritten information in *Language and Historical Representation: Getting the Story Crooked* (Madison: University of Wisconsin Press, 1989.) From 1998 until the present, an array of USC graduate students has pondered and engaged the complexities of information—particularly information and language developed and used by previously ill-considered individuals in my "The Art of Historical Writing" graduate seminar.

26. For Paz, sexual geography was limited either to an array of hotel rooms, or to the plaza in Madrid. It did not involve women's bodies as suggested here. Nor did it involve the possibility—and potential consequences—of childbirth. Yet this possibility must have been much on the minds of women, as my interviews with Rocha, which overflowed with information revealing her concerns about her son, and my conversations with the Barragán family, who sought me out in California with concerns about a daughter who had settled there, suggest. Interview with Rocha; conversations with Valadéz, Ario de Rayón; and conversation with Valadéz, Los Angeles, California, 1994.

27. Becker, *Setting the Virgin on Fire*. See also Jocelyn Olcott's insightful *Revolutionary Women in Postrevolutionary Mexico* (Durham, NC: Duke University Press, 2005).

28. Consider the intriguing approaches to space found in Mauricio Tenorio, *I Speak the City: Mexico City at the Turn of the Twentieth Century* (Chicago: University of Chicago Press, 2012); the array of important Mexican regional studies, many of which focused on Michoacán, including Luis González y González, *San José de Gracia: Mexican Village in Transition*, trans. John Upton (Austin: University of Texas Press, 1975). See too Florencia Mallon's compelling *Courage Tastes of Blood: The Mapuche Community of Nicolás Atilio and the Chilean State, 1906–2001* (Durham, NC: Duke University Press, 2005).

29. Initially, numerous northwestern Michoacán male peasants refused governmental property, as my series of interviews with Francisco Elizalde and Ignacio

Espitia revealed. Consequently, agrarian leaders including Juan Gutíerrez sought out Michoacán men with limited previous experience of farming, suggesting the economic benefits of participating in the land reform. Interview with Elizalde, June 2, 1988. Interview with Ignacio Espitia, Zamora, Michoacán, August 18, 1985.

30. While chapter one argues that the women's walks to the league meetings and the subsequent events played roles in the women's ambulatory ways of experiencing and changing history, here the exploration is into ways the women created a gendered language to describe, assess, and communicate about their engagements with time.

31. On the silencing, see Paz, *Sunstone/Piedra de Sol*. On the demands that females model experiences and expressions of purity, see Becker, *Setting the Virgin on Fire*, 14–17. Interviews with northwestern Michoacán priests revealed fashions in which area priests normalized this gendered approach to communication. Interviews with Padre Joaquin Paz, Zamora, Michoacán, August 1985; interview with Padre Joaquin Medina, Zamora, Michoacán, 1985.

32. During Michoacán's experience of what Gil Joseph long ago thoughtfully referred to as "revolution from without," not only did an array of land-tenure alterations take place, but also an idea regarding the changing use of buildings themselves began to take hold. See Joseph, *Revolution from Without: Yucatán, Mexico, and the United States, 1880–1924* (Cambridge, UK: Cambridge University Press, 1982.) On repurposing buildings, participant observation in Zamora, Morelia, Ario de Rayón, Pátzcuaro, Ocumicho, and Jarácuaro Michoacán, 1986–1993.

33. On gender-segregated male tertulias, participant observation and interviews with Hilario Reyes Garibaldi, Morelia, Michoacán, June 26, 1990; and with Constantino Murillo, Morelia, Michoacán, March 7, 1990.

34. Gutierrez's invitation to establish women's leagues was only to women. Interviews with Rocha, herself a league member, May 1990; with Verduzco de Peña, May 28, 1990; and with Rafael Ochoa González, November 5, 1990, Ario de Rayón.

35. The letters included Matilde Anguiano to Juan Gutiérrez, July 6, 1937, loose documents, Archivo Municipal de Zamora, (AMZ), Matilde Anguiano to Ing. Gustavo Martínez Baca, August 9, 1937, loose documents, AMZ.

36. Ochoa González's proclerical perspective regarding the leagues contradicted his frequent anticlerical critique of a church he considered counterrevolutionary. In some respects, he seemed startled by the sudden wave of female verbal and practical independence. Interview with Ochoa, Ario de Rayón, May 30, 1990.

37. Paz, *Sunstone/Piedra de Sol*.

38. Notwithstanding the array of transcendent approaches to Latin American gender relations, a Mexican meta-history focusing on gendered voice still seeks its scholar.

39. Interview with Méndez.

40. My interviews with Méndez prompted comments revealing her intense appreciation, even affection for the iconography and a dedication to the belief system the icons represented.

41. Some of the material they drew on for sermons has been housed in the Archivo de la Purísima Corazón, (APC) located in Zamora, Michoacán. This material includes "Carta pastoral colectiva de los prelados de la provincia de Michoacán, 1920."

42. Interview with Méndez.

43. Though both The Old and The New Testaments contain at times confusing chronologies, each depends on depictions of a deity and of men and women making their ways through time sequences that their behavior altered. See *The Holy Scriptures* (Philadephia: Jewish Publication Society of America, 1917); and *The Holy Bible* (Cleveland: World Publishing Company, n.d.).

44. According to Rocha, numerous women participated in the torching. Interview with Rocha. It was former Cardenista Carlos Martínez who initially described the torching to me in an interview in Ario de Rayón, Rayón, on September 7, 1985.

45. Interviews with Rocha, Verduzco de Peña, and Soledad Barragan.

46. Ochoa González and Soledad Barragán described aspects of northwestern Michoacán relationships between landowners, overseers, and workers on the rural estates. Interview with Ochoa González, May 11, 1990; interview with Soledad Barragán, Ario de Rayón, June 6, 1990.

47. Becker, *Setting the Virgin on Fire*.

48. For Latin Americanist scholarship relating to dance and to contexts in which dance has been politicized, see Diane Taylor, *The Archive and the Repertoire: Performing Cultural Memory in the Americas* (Durham, NC: Duke University Press, 2003), *Paul Scolierie Dancing the New World: Aztecs, Spaniards and the Choreography of Conquest* (Austin: University of Texas Press, 2013); Barbara Browning, *Samba: Resistance in Motion* (Bloomington: University of Indiana Press, 1995); and Susan Leigh Foster, *Choreographing Empathy: Kinesthesia in Performance* (Routledge: New York, 2011).

Chapter Four

1. Octavio Paz, *The Labyrinth of Solitude: Life and Thought in Mexico*, trans. Lysander Kemp (New York: Grove Press, 1961). For Paz's approach to a more just Mexico, see Paz, *The Labyrinth of Solitude*, 148–49

2. Octavio Paz, *The Other Mexico: Critique of the Pyramid*, trans. Lysander Kemp (New York: Grove Press, 1972). See also Marjorie Becker, "The Revolution and the Pyramid," seminar paper, Duke University, 1980.

3. A similar approach even emerges in Paz's biography of the seventeenth-century poet Sor Juana Inés de la Cruz. While Paz's view that Mexican misogyny limited Sor Juana's experiences as person and as poet is significant, his overly constrained approach to female sexuality limits his assessment of Sor Juana's erotic poetry. See Octavio Paz, *Sor Juana: Or, the Traps of Faith* (Cambridge, MA: Harvard University Press, 1988), 483.

4. Paz, *Labyrinth of Solitude*, 86.

5. For a thoughtful, admiring approach to Paz, see Enrique Krauze, *Redeemers: Ideas and Power in Latin America*, trans. Hank Heifetz and Natalie Wimmer (New York: Harper, 2011), 119–220.

6. Paz, *Labyrinth of Solitude*, 29–46.

7. Paz, *Labyrinth of Solitude*, 29–46.

8. Because Paz's concern was Mexican men, La Malinche emerged in his writing as little more than a pawn. For a crucial assessment of some of these issues, see Jean Franco, *Plotting Women: Gender and Representation in Mexico* (New York: Columbia University Press, 1989). For a study of modern Mexican machismo, see Mathew C. Gutman, *The Meanings of Macho: Being a Man in Mexico* City (Berkeley: University of California Press, 1995). For an insightful recent study, see Mary Kay Vaughan, *Portrait of a Painter: Pepe Zuniga and Mexico City's Rebel Generation* (Durham, NC: Duke University Press, 2015).

9. Paz, *Labyrinth of Solitude*, 86.

10. Paz, *Labyrinth of Solitude*, 86.

11. Bernal Díaz del Castillo, *The Discovery and Conquest of Mexico*, trans. A. P. Maudslay (New York: Farrar, Straus, and Cudahy, 1956), 66.

12. While assessments of La Malinche have changed and have been politically charged over time, key approaches include Camila Townsend, *Malinche's Choices: An Indian Woman in the Conquest of Mexico* (Albuquerque: University of New Mexico Press, 2006); Sandra Messenger Cypress, *La Malinche in Mexican Literature: From History to Myth* (Austin: University of Texas Press,) 1991; Franco, *Plotting Women*, Frances Karttunen, "To the Valley of Mexico: Doña Marina, 'La Malinche (ca. 1500–1527),'" in Frances Kartunnen, *Between Worlds: Interpreters, Guides and Survivors* (New Brunswick, New Jersey: Rutgers University Press, 1994). For an approach that views La Malinche as the mother of all who have populated the Western world, see Tzvetan Todorov, *The Conquest of America: The Question of the Other*, trans. Richard Howard (New York: Harper Perennial, 1984).

13. Townsend, too, considers this issue and suggests that La Malinche's recognition of the challenging context she experienced may have prompted her to reveal her knowledge of Nahuatl. See Townsend, *Malinche's Choices*, 41. See Also Sandra Messenger Cypress, *La Malinche in Mexican Literature: From History to Myth* (Austin: University of Texas Press, 1991).

14. On the Tlaxcalans and their experience of the Spanish conquest, see Charles Gibson, *Tlaxcala in the Sixteenth Century* (New Haven: Yale University Press, 1952), Inga Clendinnen, "'Fierce and Unnatural Cruelty,'" in *The Cost of Courage in Mexican Society: Essays on Mesoamerican Society and Culture* (Cambridge: Cambridge University Press, 2010), 49–90.

15. Showing no concern regarding other aspects of La Malinche's experience with Cortés, Paz also ignored the psychological and physical effects pregnancy would have imposed on her.

16. Paz, *Labyrinth of Solitude*, 39–46.

17. Paz, *Labyrinth of Solitude*, 148–49

18. Numerous scholars have considered the revolution as a series of outbursts informed by Mexican desires for a more just social order. Most particularly, these works and others have shared a depth of concern about Mexico's peasants—key revolutionary protagonists, after all—be understood in their complexity. Some of these scholarly works include Frank Tannenbaum, *The Mexican Agrarian Revolution* (New York: Archon Books, 1968); John Womack Jr., *Zapata and the Mexican Revolution* (New York: Vintage Books, 1968); Friedrich Katz, *The Life and Times of Pancho Villa* (Stanford: Stanford University Press, 1998); and Alan Knight, *The Mexican Revolution*, 2 vols. (Cambridge: Cambridge University Press, 1986). See also the forthcoming study on Frank Tannenbaum by Barbara Weinstein.

19. For an ethnohistorical definition of culture, see Marjorie Becker, *Setting the Virgin on Fire: Lázaro Cárdenas, Michoacán Peasants, and the Redemption of the Mexican Revolution* (Berkeley: University of California Press, 1996). The volume *Everyday Forms of State Formation: Revolution and the Negotiation of Rule in Modern Mexico*, edited by Gilbert M. Joseph and Daniel Nugent, has been understood as a turning point in Mexican revolutionary historiography. See *Everyday Forms of State Formation* (Durham, NC: Duke University Press, 1994). See also Daniel Nugent, *Spent Cartridges of Revolution: An Anthropological History of Namiquipa, Chihuahua* (Chicago: University of Chicago Press, 1993).

20. For a crucial monograph focusing on Zapata and his movement, see Womack, *Zapata and the Mexican Revolution*. See, too, Samuel Brunk, *Emiliano Zapata: Revolution and Betrayal in Mexico* (Albuquerque: University of New Mexico Press, 1995).

21. Paz, *Labyrinth of Solitude*, 144, 149.

22. Paz, *Labyrinth of Solitude*, 144, 149.

23. The fact that the Zapatista entry into Mexico City, a city they had won militarily, was marked by Zapatista warriors begging for food rather than taking the national palace continues to suggest key aspects of Zapatista warriors' understanding of revolution.

24. Knight, *The Mexican Revolution*.

25. See Elena Poniatowska, *Hasta no verte Jesús mio* (Mexico City: Ediciones era, 1969); Gilbert M. Joseph and Jürgen Buchenau, *Mexico's Once and Future Revolution: Social Upheaval and the Challenge of Rule since the Late Nineteenth Century* (Durham, NC: Duke University Press, 2013); Elizabeth Salas, *Soldaderas in the Mexican Military: Myth and History* (Austin: University of Texas Press, 1990); Jocelyn Olcott, "The Center Cannot Hold: Women on Mexico's Popular Front," in *Sex in Revolution: Gender, Politics, and Power in Modern Mexico*, eds. Jocelyn Olcott, Mary Kay Vaughan, and Gabriela Cano (Durham, NC: Duke University Press, 2006).

26. Elena Poniatowska created a remarkable oral history of the movement and the massacre in which she interviewed and shared the voices of an array of Mexicans involved. See her *La noche de Tlaltelolco* (Mexico DF: Ediciones Era, S.A., 1971). See, too, Elaine Carey, *Plaza of Sacrifices: Gender, Power, and Terror in 1968 Mexico* (Albuquerque: University of New Mexico Press, 2005).

27. Paz, *The Other Mexico*.

28. Paz, *The Other Mexico*, 19, 75.

29. Paz, *The Other Mexico*, 73, 74.

30. Paz, *The Other Mexico*, 74.

31. "Editorial," *Fem: publicación feminista* IV, no. 16 (September 1980–1981): 5.

32. Despite the need for more historical studies focusing on Mexican female domestic servitude, important information regarding Mexican women's experiences of servitude can be found in the Mexican journal *Fem*. In particular, see vol. 4, no. 16, which is dedicated to modern Mexican domestic service. *Fem: publicación feminista* (Mexico Df.: Nueva Cultura Feminista, 1980–1981). For an example of female servitude in colonial Mexico, see Steve J. Stern, *The Secret History of Gender: Women, Men, and Power in late Colonial Mexico* (Chapel Hill: University of North Carolina Press, 1995), 103. For an important study of Mexican immigrants whose work at times included domestic service, see Ana Miniam, *Undocumented Lives: The Untold Story of Mexican Migration* (Cambridge, MA: Harvard University Press, 2018), 122. I observed Mexican women performing multiple domestic tasks during my ethnohistorical research in Mexico City, urban and rural Michoacán, 1985–1995.

33. Elena Urrutia, "Las que sacuden y barren nuestras porfiriadas miserias," *Fem: publicación feminista* IV, no. 16 (1981): 6–9; Elena Urrutia, "Experiences de organización," *Fem: publicación feminista* IV, no. 16 (1981): 37–39. Participant observation in Zamora, Michoacán, 1990.

34. Participant observation in Zamora, Michoacán, 1990; participant observation in Ario de Rayón, Michoacán, 1990.

35. Participant observation, Zamora, Michoacán, July 1990, November 1990.

36. Interviews and participant observation with Maria Elena Verduzco de Peña, Ario de Rayón, Michoacán, April 1990, May 1990.

37. Interview with Concepción Méndez, Ario de Rayón, November 1990.

38. Carrey, *Plaza of Sacrifices*, 6; Marta Lamas, "Feminismo y organizaciones políticas de iquierda en México," *Fem: publicación feminista* V, no. 17: 35–37.

39. Elena Poniatowska, *Massacre in Mexico*, trans. Helen R. Lane (Columbia: University of Missouri Press, 1975), 217

40. Poniatowska, *Massacre in Mexico*, 92, 93.

41. Poniatowska, *Massacre in Mexico*, 155, 209, 224–26.

Coda

1. The song is entitled "Un Violador en tu camino," translated as "the rapist in your path," and has mobilized and energized women throughout the world, many of whom readily identify with its meaning.

2. The late poet and novelist Rosario Castellanos's short story "Modesta Gómez" displays another example of a Mexican woman living in a harrowing historical context that limited her choices and decisions. A victim of poverty, rape, and abandonment, Modesta Gómez chose to become an ambusher whose occupation was to rob, abuse, and intimidate Indigenous women in the state of Chiapas. See Rosario Castellanos, "Modesta Gómez," in *City of Kings*, trans. Robert S. Rudder and Gloria Chacón de Arjona, 47–55 (Claremont, CA: Svenson Publishers, 2018). Another more contemporary artist who has focused on some of the challenges some Mexican women have experienced is the filmmaker Aldolfo Cuarón, whose renowned film *Roma* focuses on the courage and frequent silence of the servant Cleo, who risked her own life to save the lives of her employers' children.

3. Rosario Castellanos, "Modesta Gómez."

4. Castellanos, "Modesta Gómez," 47–48.

5. Castellanos, "Modesta Gómez," 47–48.

6. Castellanos, "Modesta Gómez," 51.

7. Castellanos, "Modesta Gómez," 49.

8. Castellanos, "Modesta Gómez," 52.

9. Castellanos, "Modesta Gómez," 53.

10. Castellanos, "Modesta Gómez," 55.

11. Numerous scholars, writers, and film critics have assessed this movie, usually to deep acclaim. For an example, see Ilan Stavans, "In *Roma*, Alfonso Cuarón Zooms in on Class Tensions," *In These Times*, December 5, 2018.

12. Alvaro Cuarón, *Roma*.

13. Cuarón, *Roma*.

14. While Cuarón's development of Cleo can be viewed as that of a privileged filmmaker's belated recognition of the contours of a system that mainly valued

wealth, skin tone, and position to the detriment of the rest of Mexico's population, his depiction of Cleo's complex responses to her experiences—and, as I argue here—her complicated verbal expressions of them, can be understood as an outsider's empathic attempt to view the world through her eyes. There have been numerous scholarly responses to the film. Some of the most interesting include Ilan Stavans, "In *Roma*, Alfonso Cuarón Zooms in on Class Tensions," *In these Times*, December 5, 2018.

15. See Sophia Koutsoyannis, "Background Paper: Femicide in Ciudad Juarez. Ever-Present and Worsening," October 2011.

16. These words are from the feminist anthem created by the Chilean group Las Tesis and performed throughout the world in response to persistent assaults against women. See Gaby Hinsliff, "'The Rapist Is You!' Why A Chilean Protest Chant Is Being Sung Around the World," *The Guardian*, February 3, 2020, https://www.theguardian.com/society/2020/feb/03/the-rapist-is-you-chilean-protest-song-chanted-around-the-world-un-iolador-en-tu-camino. See also Alma Guillermoprieto, "Letters from Mexico: One Hundred Women," *New Yorker*, September 29, 2003, https://www.newyorker.com/magazine/2003/09/29/a-hundred-women.

BIBLIOGRAPHY

Primary Sources

ARCHIVES

Mexico City

Archivo General de la Nación, Fondo Presidentes
Lázaro Cárdenas
Archivo Histórico de la Secretaría de Educación Pública
Archivo Histórico de la Secretaría de Reforma Agraria
Hemeroteca de la Ciudad Universitaria

Morelia

Archivo General de Poder Ejecutivo de Michoacán
Archivo Histórico Manuel Castañeda Ramírez
Archivo Judicial del Estado de Michoacán
Archivo del Poder Judicial
Archivo de la Secretaría de Reforma Agraria

Zamora

Archivo Municipal de Zamora
Archivo Particular de Juan Gutiérrez
Archivo Particular de José Lomeli
Archivo de la Purísima Corazón

PUBLISHED DOCUMENTS

Eliot, T. S. *Four Quartets*. San Diego: Harcourt Inc., 1943.
———. *The Waste Land*. New York: Norton Critical Edition, 2001.
Hughes, Ted. *Crow: From the Life and Songs of the Crow*. London: Faber and Faber, 1972.
Neruda, Pablo. *Canto General*. Translated by Jack Schmitt. Berkeley: University of California Press, 1991.

———. *The Essential Neruda: Selected Poems*. Edited by Mark Eisner. San Francisco: City Lights Books, 2004.

———. Neruda, Pablo. "I explain a few things." In *The FSG Book of Twentieth Century Latin American Poetry*, edited by Ilan Stavans, 266–72. New York: Farrar, Strauss and Giroux, 2011.

———. *Selected Odes*. Translated by Margaret Sayers Peden. Berkeley: University of California Press, 1990.

———. *Selected Poems*. Edited by Nathaniel Tarn. London: Vintage Books, 2012.

———. *Twenty Love Poems and a Song of Despair*. Translated by W. S. Merwin. New York: Penguin, 2006.

Paz, Octavio. *The Collected Poems of Octavio Paz, 1957–1987*. Edited by Eliot Weinberger. New York: New Directions, 1987.

———. *Configurations*. Translated by Muriel Rukeyser et. al. New York: New Directions, 1971.

———. *Labyrinth of Solitude: Life and Thought in Mexico*. Translated by Lysander Kemp. New York: Grove Press, 1961.

———. *The Other Mexico: Critique of the Pyramid*. Translated by Lysander Kemp. New York: Grove Press: 1972.

———. *Pasión Crítica*. Barcelona: Editorial Seix Barral Biblioteca Breve, 1985.

———. *La búsqueda del presente:1990 Conferencia Nobel/In Search of the Present: 1990 Nobel Lecture*. San Diego, New York, Harcourt Brace Jovanovich, Publishers, 1990.

———. *Sunstone: Piedra de Sol*. Translated by Eliot Weinberger. New York: New Directions, 1991.

INTERVIEWS

Aceves, Celso. Ario de Rayón, Michoacán. May 15, 1990.

Aceves, Jesús. Ario de Rayón, Michoacán. May 15, 1990.

Acosta, Angelina. Zamora, Michoacán. November 8, 1990.

Amezcua, Luis. Ario de Rayón, Michoacán. May 28, 1990.

Arreola Cortéz, Raul. Mexico City. August 20, 1984.

Barragán, Soledad. Ario de Rayón, Michoacán. June 6, 1990.

Capilla, Eulario. Jarácuaro, Michoacán. September 2, 1985.

Cervantes, Carlos. Ario de Rayón, Michoacán. June 7, 1990.

Corona Nuñez, José. Morelia, Michoacán. July 12, 1985; July 11, 1989.

Elizalde, Francisco. Zamora, Michoacán. July 19, 26, 1985; June 2, 1988; November 5, 1990.

Espitia, Ignacio. Zamora, Michoacán. August 18, 25, 1985.

Garibay, Luis. Zamora, Michoacán. August 23, 1985

Godínez López, Francisco. Ario de Rayón. May 1, 1990.

González Esquivel, Francisco. Zamora, Michoacán. August 5, 1985.

Lomelí, José. Zamora, Michoacán. August 20, 26, 1985.

López, Atiliano. Jarácuaro, Michoacán. August 31, 1985.

Losornio, Enrique. Zamora, Michoacán. August 24, 1985.

Martínez, Carlos. Ario de Rayón, Michoacán. December 7, 1985.

Mayes, Julia. Morelia, Michoacán. December 8, 1985.

Mayes Navarro, Antonio. Morelia, Michoacán. December 4, 1984.

Medina, Padre Porfirio. Zamora, Michoacán. August 12, 1985.

Miranda, Padre Francisco. Zamora, Michoacán. March 15, 1990.

Múgica Martínez, Jesús. Morelia, Michoacán. December 4, 1984; July 11, 1988; July 10, 1989; August 3, 1989; June 26, 1990; August 3, 1990.

Murillo, Constantino. Morelia, Michoacán. July 16, 1985; March 7, 1990.

Ochoa González, Rafael. Ario de Rayón, Michoacán. May 7, 11, 12 1990; July 13, 1990; November 5, 1990.

Padilla, Maximino. Zamora, Michoacán. August 16, 1985.

Paz, Padre Joaquín. Zamora, Michoacán. August 12, 1985.

Peña, Salvador. Ario de Rayón, Michoacán. September 6, 1985.

Pérez, Vicente. Zamora, Michoacán. August 8, 1985.

Ramirez, Celerino. Jarácuaro, Michoacán. September 2, 1985.

Reyes Garibaldi, Hilario. Morelia, Michoacán. July 18, 1985; June 26, 1990.

Rico Cano, Tomás. Morelia, Michoacán. June 26, 1990; August 3, 1990.

Río, Santiago del. Zamora, Michoacán. August 22, 1985.

Rocha, Esperanza. Ario de Rayón, Michoacán. May 13, 1990; June 2, 1990; July 6, 1990.

Valadéz de García, Carmen. Ario de Rayón, Michoacán. June 9, 1990.

Valencia Ayala, Francisco. Zamora, Michoacán. August 13, 1985.

Verduzco de Peña, Mari Elena. Ario de Rayón. April 24, 25, 27, 28, 30, 1990; May 25, 27, 1990; July 12, 1990; November 1, 1990.

Villaseñor Espinosa, Roberto. Mexico City. March 1, 1984.

Secondary Sources

Arrom, Silvia. *Containing the Poor: The Mexico City Poorhouse, 1774–1871*. Durham, NC: Duke University Press, 2001.

———. *La Guerra Rodríguez: The Life and Legends of a Mexican Independence Heroine*. Berkeley: University of California Press, 2021.

———. *The Women of Mexico City, 1790–1857*. Stanford: Stanford University Press, 1985.

Aviña, Alex. *Specters of Revolution: Peasant Guerrillas in the Cold War Mexican Countrywide*. Oxford: Oxford University Press, 2016.

Barthes, Roland. *The Grain of the Voice: Interviews 1962–1980.* Translated by Linda Coverdale. New York: Hill and Wang, 1985.

Bartra, Roger. *La jaula de melancolía: Identidad y Metamorfosis del mexicano.* Mexico City: Editorial Grijalbo, 1987.

Bauer, Arnold. *Goods, Power, History: Latin American Material Culture.* Cambridge: Cambridge University Press, 2010.

Bazant, Milada. *Laura Mendez de Cuenca: Mexican Feminist, 1853–1928.* Tucson: University of Arizona Press, 2018.

Becker, Marjorie. "As though they meant her no harm, María Enríquez remade the friends who abandoned her—their possibilities, their worlds—inviting them (perhaps, it is true) to dance." *Rethinking History: The Journal of Theory and Practice.* 12, no. 2 (June 2008): 153–64.

———. *Body Bach.* Huntington Beach: Tebot Bach, 2005.

———. *The Macon Sex School: Songs of Tenderness and Resistance.* Huntington Beach: Tebot Bach, 2020.

———. "Music, Such Sudden Music: When Mexican Women Altered Space in Time," *Rethinking History: The Journal of Theory and Practice* 23, no. 1 (March 2019): 2–15.

———. *Piano Glass/Glass Piano.* Huntington Beach: Tebot Bach, 2010.

———. "The Revolution and the Pyramid: A Critique of Octavio Paz." Seminar Paper, Duke University, 1980.

———. *Setting the Virgin on Fire: Lázaro Cárdenas, Michoacán Peasants and the Redemption of the Mexican Revolution.* Berkeley: University of California Press, 1995.

———. "Talking Back to Frida: Houses of Emotional Mestizaje." *History and Theory* 41 (December 2002): 56–71.

———. "Torching La Purísima, Dancing at the Altar: The Construction of Revolutionary Hegemony in Michoacán, 1934–1940." In *Everyday Forms of State Formation: Revolution and the Negotiation of Rule in Modern Mexico,* edited by Gilbert M. Joseph and Daniel Nugent, 247–64. Durham: Duke University Press, 1994.

———. "When I Was a Child, I Danced as a Child, but Now that I am Old, I Think about Salvation: Concepción González and a past that would not stay put." *Rethinking History: The Journal of Theory and Practice* 1, no. 3 (Winter 1997): 343–56.

———. "You Grabbed Me as Though You Owned My Body, But I'm Here to Say You're Wrong: Toward a Letter to the Zamora Sexual Assailant." *Rethinking History: The Journal of Theory and Practice,* 2021.

Behar, Ruth. *Translated Woman: Crossing the Border with Esperanza's Story.* Boston: Beacon Press, 1993.

Berger, Miriam. "Women in Mexico are protesting femicide. Police have responded with force." *Washington Post*, March 9, 2021, https://www.washingtonpost.com/world/2021/03/09/womens-day-protests-amlo-mexico/.

Bidart, Frank. *The Sacrifice*. New York: Vintage Books, 1993.

Bloom, Harold, ed. *Octavio Paz*. Philadelphia: Chelsea House Publications, 2001.

Bonfil Batalla, Guillermo. *Mexico Profundo: Reclaiming a Civilization*. Translated by Philip A. Dennis. Austin: University of Texas Press, 1996.

Brading, David. *Octavio Paz y la poesía de la historia mexicana*. Mexico City: Fondo de cultura económica, 2004.

Browning, Barbara. *Samba: Resistance in Motion*. Bloomington: Indiana University Press, 1995.

Brunfiel, Elizabeth. "Weaving and Cooking: Women Production in Aztec Mexico." In *Engendering Archeology: Women and Prehistory*, edited by Joan M. Gero and Margaret W. Conkey, 224–51. Oxford: Blackwell.

Brunk, Samuel. *Emiliano Zapata: Revolution and Betrayal in Mexico*. Albuquerque: University of New Mexico Press, 1995.

Burns, Kathryn. *Colonial Habits: Convents and the Spiritual Economy of Cuzco, Peru*. Durham, NC: Duke University Press, 1999.

Callan, Richard J. *The Philosophy of Yoga in Octavio Paz's Poem BLANCO*. Leviston, New York: The Edwin Mellen Press, 2005.

Cameron, Sharon. *Lyric Time: Dickinson and the Limits of Genre*. Baltimore: The Johns Hopkins University Press, 1979.

Caiser, Nick. *Octavio Paz*. London: Reaktion Book, Ltd. 2007.

Caparnos, Martín. "Juan Rulfo: 'Los Latinoamericanos están pensando todo el día en el muerte.'" *New York Times*, May 15, 2012, https://www.nytimes.com/es/2017/05/15/espanol/opinion/juan-rulfo-centenario-caparros.html.

Carrey, Elaine. *Plaza de Sacrifices: Gender, Power, and Terror in 1968 Mexico*. Albuquerque: University of New Mexico Press, 2005.

Castellanos, Rosario. *City of Kings*. Translated by Robert S. Rudder and Gloria Chacón de Arjona. Claremont, CA: Svenson, 2018.

———. *Ciudad Real*. Jalapa, Mexico: Universidad Verecruzana, 1982.

Chowning, Margaret. *Rebellious Nun: The Troubled History of a Mexican Convent, 1954–1863*. Oxford: Oxford University Press, 2006.

Clendinnen, Inga. *Aztecs: An Interpretation*. Cambridge, UK: Cambridge University Press, 1991.

———. *Ambivalent Conquests: Maya and Spaniard in Yucatan, 1517–1570*. Cambridge, UK: Cambridge University Press, 1987.

———. "Fierce and Unnatural Cruelty." In *The Cost of Courage in Mesoamerican Society*, edited by Inga Clendinnen, 6–48. Cambridge: Cambridge University Press, 2010.

Coatsworth, John. "Railroads, Landholding and Agrarian Protest in the Early Porfiriato." *Hispanic American Historical Review* 57 (1974): 48–71.

Cuarón, Alfonso, *Roma*. Mexico City: Espectáculas Fílmicos El Coyúl, 2018.

Cypress, Sandra Messenger. *La Malinche in Mexican Literature: From History to Myth*. Austin: University of Texas Press, 1991.

———. *Uncivil Wars: Elena Garro, Octavio Paz and the Battle for Cultural Memory*. Austin: University of Texas Press, 2012.

Dávila, Marisol, and Marisol LaBron, "'Un Violador en tu camino' and the Virality of Feminist Protest." *Nacla*, December 27, 2019, https://nacla.org/news/2019/12/27/un-violador-en-tu-camino-virality-feminist-protest.

Dawson, Alex. *Indian and Nation in Revolutionary Mexico*. Tucson: University of Arizona Press, 2004.

Depar, Helen. *The Emotional Vogue of Things Mexican: Cultural Relations between the U.S. and Mexico, 1920–1935*. Tuscaloosa: University of Alabama Press, 1992.

Diamond, Jared. *Guns, Germs, and Steel: The Fate of Human Societies*. New York: Norton, 1997.

Díaz del Castillo, Bernal. *The Discovery and Conquest of Mexico*. Translated by A. P. Maudslay. New York: Farra, Straus, and Cudahy, 1956.

Fein, John. *Toward Octavio Paz: A Reading of His Major Poems, 1957–1976*. Lexington: University Press of Kentucky, 1986.

Fernández Aceves, Maria Teresa. "Advocate or Cacica? Guadalupe Urzúa Flores: Modernizer and Peasant Political Leader in Jalisco." In *Dictablanda: Politics, Work, and Culture in Mexico, 1938–1968*, edited by Paul Gillingham and Benjamin Smith, 236–54. Durham, NC: Duke University Press, 2014.

Findlay, Eileen J. Suarez. *We Are Left without a Father Here: Masculinity, Domesticity and Migration in Postwar Puerto Rico*. Durham, NC: Duke University Press, 2014.

Flores, Angel. *Aproximaciones a Octavio Paz*. Mexico City: Joaquin Mortiz, 1974.

Florescano, Enrique. *Memory, Myth and Time: From the Aztecs to Independence*. Translated by Albert G. Bork and Katherine R. Bork. Austin: University of Texas Press, 1994.

Foster, Susan Leigh. *Choreographing Empathy: Kinesthesia in Performance*. London: Routledge, 2011.

Fowler-Salamini, Heather. *Working Women, Entrepreneurs, and the Mexican Revolution: The Coffee Culture of Cordoba, Veracruz*. Lincoln: University of Nebraska Press, 2020.

Fowler-Salamini Heather, and Mary Kay Vaughan. *Women of the Mexican Countryside, 1850–1940: Creating Spaces, Shaping Transitions*. Tucson: University of Arizona Press, 1994.

Franco, Jean. *An Introduction to Spanish American Literature*. Cambridge: Cambridge University Press, 1994.

———. *Cruel Modernity*. Durham, NC: Duke University Press, 2013.

———. *Plotting Women: Gender and Representation in Mexico*. New York: Columbia University Press, 1990.

Frazier, Lessie Jo. *Desired States: Sex, Gender, and Political Culture in Chile* (New Brunswick: Rutgers University Press, 2020.

Friedrich, Paul. *The Princes of Naranja: An Essay in Anthrohistorical Method*. Austin: University of Texas Press, 1986.

Fuentes, Carlos. "Mexico and Its Demons." *New York Review of Books*, September 20, 1973.

García Márquez, Gabriel, *Chronicles of a Death Foretold*. Translated Gregory Rabassa. New York: Vintage, 2003.

Garro, Elena. *Memorias de España 1937*. Mexico City: Siglo XXI Editores, 1992.

Garman, Emma. "Feminize Your Canon: Rosario Castellanos." *The Paris Review*, September 17, 2018, https://www.theparisreview.org/blog/2018/09/17/feminize-your-canon-rosario-castellanos/.

Gibson, Charles. *The Aztecs under Spanish Rule: A History of the Indians of the Valley of Mexico, 1519–1810*. Stanford: Stanford University Press, 1964.

———. *Tlaxcala in the Sixteenth Century*. New Haven: Yale University Press, 1952.

González y González, Luis, ed. *Historia de la Revolución Mexicana*. Vol 6, no. 15, *Los días del Presidente Cárdenas*. Mexico: El Colegio de Meciso, 1981.

———. *San José de Gracia: Mexican Village in Transition*. Translated by John Upton. Austin: University of Texas Press, 1975.

———. *Zamora*. Zamora: El Colegio de Michoacán/Conacyt, 1984.

Goodman, James. *But Where Is the Lamb? Imagining the Story of Abraham and Isaac*. New York: Schocken Books, 2013.

Griffin, Susan. *Woman and Nature: The Roaring Inside Her*. New York: Harper and Row, Publishers, 1978.

Guillermoprieto, Alma. "Letter from Mexico: One Hundred Women." *New Yorker*, September 29, 2003, https://www.newyorker.com/magazine/2003/09/29/a-hundred-women.

———. "The Return of Macho Politics?" *New Yorker*, February 24, 2010, https://www.newyorker.com/news/news-desk/the-return-of-macho-politics .

Gutman, Matthew C. *The Meanings of Macho: Being a Man in Mexico City*. Berkeley: University of California Press, 1995.

Hall, Donald. *Goatfoot, Milktongue, Twinbird: Interviews, Essays and Notes on Poetry, 1970–76*. Ann Arbor: University of Michigan Press, 1978.

Heath, Charles V. *The Inevitable Bandstand: The State Band of Oaxcaca and the Politics of Sound*. Lincoln: University of Nebraska Press, 2015.

Hinsliff, Gaby. "'The Rapist Is You!': Why A Chilean Protest Chant Is Being Sung Around the World." *The Guardian*, February 3, 2020, https://www.theguardian.com/society/2020/feb/03/the-rapist-is-you-chilean-protest-song-chanted-around-the-world-un-iolador-en-tu-camino.

——. *The Holy Bible*. Cleveland: World Publishing Company, n.d.

——. *The Holy Scriptures*. Philadelphia: Jewish Publication Society of America, 1917.

Horn, Rebecca. *Postconquest Coyoacan: Nahua-Spanish Relations in Central Mexico, 1519–1650*. Stanford: Stanford University Press, 1997.

Isolde Roque Paillalef, Rosa. *When a Flower is Reborn: The Life and Times of a Mapuche Feminist*. Edited and translated by Florencia Mallon. Durham, NC: Duke University Press, 2002.

Jackson, Gabriel. *A Concise History of the Spanish Civil War*. London: Thames and Hudson Limited, 1974.

Joseph, Gilbert M., and Daniel Nugent, eds. *Everyday Forms of State Formation: Revolution and the Negotiation of Rule in Modern Mexico*. Durham, NC: Duke University Press, 1994.

Joseph, Gilbert, and Jürgen Buchenau. *Mexico's Once and Future Revolution: Social Upheaval and the Challenge of Rule since the Late Nineteenth Century*. Durham, NC: Duke University Press, 2013.

Joseph, Gilbert. *Revolution from Without: Yucatan, Mexico and the United States, 1880–1924*. Cambridge, UK: Cambridge University Press, 1982.

Kandell, Jonathon. "Octavio Paz, Mexico's Man of Letters, Dies at 84." *New York Times*, April 21, 1988.

Kaplan, Temma. "Gender on the Barricades." *Journal of Women's History* 9, no. 3 (Autumn 1997): 177–85.

Karttunen, Frances. *Between Worlds: Interpreters, Guides, and Survivors*. New Brunswick, Rutgers University Press, 1994.

——. "To the Valley of Mexico: Doña Marina, 'La Malinche' (ca. 1500–1527)." In *Between Worlds: Interpreters, Guides, and Survivors: Interpreters, Guides and Survivors*, 1–23. New Brunswick, Rutgers University Press, 1994.

——. "Rethinking Malinche." In *Indian Women of Early Mexico*, edited by Susan Schroeder, Stephanie Wood, and Robert Haskett, 291–312. Norman: University of Oklahoma Press, 1997.

Katz, Friedrich. "Labor Conditions on Haciendas in Porfirian Mexico: Some Trends and Tendencies." *Hispanic American Historical Review* 57 (1974): 1–47.

——. *The Life and Times of Pancho Villa*. Stanford: Stanford University Press: 1998.

Katzew, Ilona. *Casta Painting: Images or Race in Eighteenth Century Mexico*. New Haven: Yale University Press, 2004.

Kellner, Hans. *Language and Historical Representation: Getting the Story Crooked*. Madison: University of Wisconsin Press, 1979.

Knight, Alan. "Cardenismo: Juggernaut or Jalopy." *Journal of Latin American Studies* 26, no. 1 (February 2004): 73–107.

———. *The Mexican Revolution*. 2 vols. Cambridge, UK: Cambridge University Press, 1986.

Koutsoyannis, Sophie. "Background Paper: Femicide in Ciudad Juarez. Ever-Present and Worsening." October 2011.

Krause, Enrique. *Redeemers: Ideas and Power in Latin America*. Translated Hank Heifetz and Natasha Wimmer. New York: Harper, 2011.

Kripner Martínez, James. *Rereading the Conquest: The History of Early Colonial Michoacán, 1521–1565*. University Park: Penn State University Press, 2001.

Lamos, Marta, "Feminismo y organizaciones políticos izquierda en Mexico." *Fem: Publicación feminista* V, no. 17 (February–March 1981): 35–37.

Levine, Philip. *The Bread of Time: Toward an Autobiography*. New York: Alfred A. Knopf, 1995.

———. *Don't Ask*. Ann Arbor: University of Michigan Press, 1981.

———. *So Ask: Essays, Conversations, and Interviews*. Ann Arbor: University of Michigan Press, 2005.

Lewis, Oscar. *Five Families: Mexican Case Studies in the Culture of Poverty*. New York: Basic Books, 1959.

Lockhart, James. *The Nahuas after the Conquest: A Social and Cultural History of the Indian of Central Mexico, Sixteenth through Eighteenth Centuries*. Stanford: Stanford University Press, 1882.

Lomnitz, Claudio. *Death and the Idea of Mexico*. New York: Zone Books, 2005.

———. "El ensayista en su centenario," *Nexos*, January 1, 2014.

Lopez Velarde, Ramon. *La Suave Patria y Otros poemas*. Mexico DF: Fondo de cultura económica, 1983.

Lumpkin, Katharine Du Pre. *The Making of a Southerner*. Westport: Greenwood Press, 1971.

MacAdam, Alfred. "Octavio Paz, The Art of Poetry No. 42." *Paris Review*, no. 119 (Summer 1991).

Mallon, Florencia. *Beyond the Ties of Blood: A Novel*. New York: Pegasus Press, 2012.

———. *Courage Tastes of Blood: The Mapuche Community of Nicolas Atilio and the Chilean State, 1906–2001*. Durham, NC: Duke University Press, 2005.

———. "Exploring the Origins of Democratic Patriarchy in Mexico: Gender and Popular Resistance in the Puebla Highlands, 1850–1876." In *Women of the*

Mexican Countryside, 1850–1990, edited by Heather Fowler-Salamini and Mary Kay Vaughan, 3–26. Tucson: University of Arizona Press, 1994.

———. *Peasant and Nation: The Making of Postcolonial Mexico and Peru.* Berkeley: University of California Press, 1995.

———. "Reflections on the Ruins: Everyday Form of State Formation in Nineteenth Century Mexico." In *Everyday Forms of State Formation*, edited by Gilbert M. Joseph and Daniel Nugent, 69–106. Durham, NC: Duke University Press, 1994.

Manahan, Patrick, *Dreaming with his Eyes Open: A Life of Diego Rivera.* New York: Alfred W. Knopt, 1998.

Marcus, Joyce. *Mesoamerican Writing Systems: Propaganda, Myth, and History in Four Ancient Civilizations.* Princeton, NJ: Princeton University Press, 1992.

Martínez, María Elena, *Genealogical Fictions: Limpieza de Sangre, Religion and Gender in Colonial Mexico.* Stanford: Stanford University Press, 2008.

Meyer, Jean. *La Cristiada.* Translated by Aurelio Garzon del Camino. 3 vols. Mexico City: Siglo XXI Editores, 1974.

———. "An Idea of Mexico: Catholicism in the Revolution." In *The Eagle and the Virgin: Nation and Cultural Revolution in Mexico, 1920–1940*, edited by Mary Kay Vaughan and Stephen E. Lewis, 281–96. Durham, NC: Duke University Press, 2006.

Minian, Ana Raquel. *Undocumented Lives: The Untold Story of Mexican Migration.* Cambridge, MA: Harvard University Press, 2018.

Monsiváis, Carlos. "When Gender Can't Be Seen Amidst the Symbols: Women and the Mexican Revolution." In *Gender, Politics, and Power in Modern Mexico*, edited by Jocelyn Olcott, Mary Kay Vaughan, and Gabriela Cano, 1–20. Durham, NC: Duke University Press, 2006.

———. "Paz, Monsiváis Polémica," *Nexos*, July 27, 1910.

Montañez, Camila. "The Green Handkerchief: The New Symbol of the International Women's Resistance." IPPF/WHR, March 8, 2019.

Needleman, Ruth. "Poetry and the Reader." In *The Perpetual Present: The Poetry and Prose of Octavio Paz*, edited by Ivar Ivask, 35–43. Norman: University of Oklahoma Press, 1973.

Norget, Kristin. *Days of Death, Days of Life: Ritual in the Popular Culture of Oaxaca.* New York: Columbia University Press, 2006.

Nugent, Daniel. *Spent Cartridges of Revolution: An Anthropological History of Namiquipa Chihuahua.* Chicago: University of Chicago Press, 1993.

Veronica Oikion "Cuca García: trazando el surco socialista a través de la Educación," *Signos Históricos* vol. 17, no. 34, Mexico, Jul/Dic, 2015.

Olcott, Jocelyn. "The Center Cannot Hold: Women on Mexico's Popular Front," in Olcott, Vaughan and Cano, eds. *Sex in Revolution*, 223–40.

———. *International Women's Year: The Greatest Consciousness-Raising Event in History*. (New York: Oxford University Press, 2017.)

———. *Revolutionary Women in Postrevolutionary Mexico*. Durham: Duke University Press, 2005.

Orwell, George. *Homage to Catalonia*. New York: Harcourt Brace and World, Inc. 1952.

Pacheco, José Emilio. "Descripción de Piedra de Sol." In *Aproximaciones a Octavio Paz*, edited by Angel Flores, 173–83. Mexico City: Joaquin Mortiz, 1974.

Paz, Octavio. *Sor Juana or the Traps of Faith*. Translated by Margaret Sayers Peden. Cambridge: Harvard University Press, 1988.

Phillips, Rachel. "Marina/Malinche: Masks and Shadow." In *Women in Hispanic Literature: Icons and Fallen Idols*, edited by Beth Miller, 97–114. Berkeley: University of California Press, 1983.

———. *The Poetic Modes of Octavio Paz*. London: Oxford University Press, 1972.

Phillips, Tom. "'This Is Our Feminist Spring': Millions of Mexican Women Decide to Strike over Femicide." *The Guardian*, March 7, 2020, https://www.theguardian.com/world/2020/mar/07/mexico-femicides-protest-women-strike.

Pilcher, Jeffrey. *¡Que Vivan los Tamales! Food and the Making of Mexican Identity*. Albuquerque: University of New Mexico Press, 1998.

Poniatowska, Elena. *Hasta no verte Jesús mío*. Mexico City: Ediciones era, 1969.

———. *Luz y Luna; Las lunitas*. Mexico DF: Ediciones era, 1994.

———. *Massacre in Mexico*. Translated by Helen R. Lane, 1975.

———. *La noche de Tlaltelolco*. Mexico DF: Ediciones era, S.A., 1971.

———. *Octavio Paz; Las palabras del arbol*. Barcelona: Plaza y Janes, Editores, 1998.

Porter, Susie, *From Angel to Office Worker: Middle-Class Identity and Female Consciousness in Mexico, 1890–1950*. Lincoln: University of Nebraska Press, 2018.

———. *Working Women in Mexico City: Public Discourses and Material Conditions, 1879–1931*. Tucson: University of Arizona Press, 2003.

Preminger, Alex, and T. V. F. Brogan, eds. "Oral Poetry." In *The New Princeton Encyclopedia of Poetry and Poetics*, 862–66. Princeton, NJ: Princeton University Press, 1993.

Premo, Bianca. *Children of the Father King: Youth, Authority and Colonial Minority in Colonial Lima, 1650–1820*. Chapel Hill: University of North Carolina Press, 2005.

———. *The Enlightenment on Trial: Ordinary Litigants and Colonialism in the Spanish Empire*. New York: Oxford University Press, 2017.

Ramos, Jorge. "In Mexico, Women Break the Silence against Femicide." *New York Times*, March 6, 2020, nytimes.com/2020/03/06/opinion/international-world/mexico-femicides-amlo.html.

Ramos, Samuel. *Profile of Man and Culture in Mexico*. Translated by Peter G. Earle. Austin: University of Texas Press, 1972.

Rappaport, Joanne, and Tom Cummins. *Beyond the Lettered City: Indigenous Literacies in the Andes*. Durham, NC: Duke University Press, 2012.

Restall, Matthew. *Seven Myths of the Spanish Conquest*. New York: Oxford University Press, 2003.

Richlin, Amy. *Arguments with Silence: Writing History of Roman Women*. Ann Arbor: University of Michigan Press, 2017.

Rodríguez Ledesma, Xavier. *El pensamiento Político de Octavio Paz: Las trampas de la ideología*. Mexico DF: Plaza y Valdés, S.A. de C.V., 1966.

Rosenstone, Robert. *Crusade of the Left: The Lincoln Brigades in the Spanish Civil War*. New York: Pegasus. 1969.

———. *The Man Who Swam into History: The (Mostly) True Story of my Jewish Family*. Austin: University of Texas Press, 2005.

———. *The Mirror in the Shrine: American Encounters in Meiji Japan*. Cambridge, MA: Harvard University Press, 1988.

Rubenstein, Anne, and Victor M. Macias Gonzalez, eds., *Masculinity and Sexuality in Modern Mexico*. Albuquerque: University of New Mexico Press, 2012.

Rukeyser, Muriel. *The Collected Poems of Muriel Rukeyser*. Edited by Janet E. Kaufman and Anne E. Herzog. Pittsburgh: University of Pittsburgh Press, 2005.

Saenz, Moises. *Carapan*. Morelia, Michoacán: Talleres Linotipograifca del gobierno del estado, 1969.

Salas, Elizabeth. *Soldaderas in the Mexican Military: Myth and History*. Austin: University of Texas Press, 1990.

Sanders, Nicole, *Gender and Welfare in Mexico: The Consolidation of a Postrevolutionary State*. University Park: Penn State University Press, 2011.

Schroeder, Susan, Stephanie Wood, and Robert Haskett, eds. *Indian Women of Early Mexico*. Norman: University of Oklahoma Press, 1997.

Scolieri, Paul. *Dancing the New World*. Austin: University of Texas Press, 2013.

Scott, James C. Foreword to *Everyday Forms of State Formation*, edited by Gilbert M. Joseph and Daniel Nugent, vii–xii. Durham: Duke University Press, 1994.

———. *Weapons of the Weak: Everyday Forms of Peasant Resistance*. New Haven: Yale University Press, 1985.

Servotte, Herman, and Ethel Greene, *Annotations of T.S. Eliot's Four Quartets*. Bloomington, IN: iUniverse, 2010.

Soustelle, Jacques. *Daily Life of the Aztecs on the Eve of the Spanish Conquest*. Translated from the French by Patrick O'Brian. Stanford: Stanford University Press, 1961.

Spivak, Gayatin Chakravorry. "How Do We Write Now?" *PMLA* 133, no. 1 (January 2018): 166–78.

Stavans, Ilan, ed. *FSG Book of Twentieth Century Latin American Poetry*. New York: Farrar, Strauss, and Giroux, 2011.

———. "In *Roma*, Alfonso Cuarón Zooms in on Class Tensions." *In These Times*, December 5, 2018, https://inthesetimes.com/article/alfonso-cuaron-middle-class-tension-film-roma-cleo-halconazo.

———. *Octavio Paz: A Meditation*. Tucson: University of Arizona Press, 2004.

Stern, Steve J. *The Secret History of Gender: Women, Men and Power in Late Colonial Mexico*. Chapel Hill: University of North Carolina Press, 1995.

Tannenbaum, Frank. *The Mexican Agrarian Revolution*. New York: Archon Books, 1968.

Taylor, Diana. *The Archive and the Repertoire: Performing Cultural Memory in the Americas*. Durham: Duke University Press, 2003.

Tenorio-trillo, Mauricio. *I Speak of the City: Mexico City at the Turn of the Twentieth Century*. Chicago: University of Chicago Press, 2012.

Thomas, Hugh. *The Spanish Civil War*. New York: Harper and Row Publishers, 1961.

Todorov, Tzvetan. *The Conquest of America: The Question of the Other*. Translated by Richard Howard. New York: Harper Perennial, 1984.

Townsend, Camila. *Malintzin's Choices: An Indian Woman in the Conquest of Mexico*. Albuquerque: University of New Mexico Press, 2006.

Uruttia, Matilde. *My Life with Pablo Neruda*. Translated by Alexandria Guardino. Stanford: Stanford University Press, 2004.

Urruttia, Elena. "Experiencias de organización." *Fem: publicación feminista* IV, no. 16 (1981): 37–39.

———. "Las que sacuden y barren nuestras porfiriados misérias." *Fem: publicación feminista* IV, no. 16 (1981): 6–9.

Vaughan, Mary Kay. *Cultural Politics in Revolution: Teachers, Peasants and the Schools in Mexico, 1930–1940*. Tucson: University of Arizona Press, 1997.

———. *Portrait of a Young Painter: Pepe Zuniga and Mexico City's Rebel Generation*. Durham, NC: Duke University Press, 2015.

Vaughan, Mary Kay, "Modernizing Patriarchy: State Policies, Rural Households and Women in Mexico, 1934–1940," in Elizabeth Dore and Maxine Molyneax, *Hidden Histories of Gender and the State in Latin America*. Durham: Duke University Press, 2000.

Vaughan, Mary Kay, and Stephen E. Lewis, eds. *The Eagle and the Virgin: Cultural Revolution in Mexico, 1920–1940*. Durham, NC: Duke University Press, 2006.

Vierba, Ezer. *The Singer's Needle: An Undisciplined History of Panamá*. Chicago: University of Chicago Press, 2021.

Villegas Muñoz, Griselda. *Emilia, una mujer de Jiquilpan.* Jiquilpan: Centro de
Estudios de la Revolución Mexicana, Lázaro Cárdenas, A.C., 1984.

White, Hayden, *Metahistory: The Historical Imagination in Nineteenth-Century
Europe.* Baltimore: The Johns Hopkins University Press, 1973.

——. *Tropics of Discourse: Essays in Cultural Criticism.* Baltimore: The Johns
Hopkins University Press, 1978.

Wilson, Jason. *Octavio Paz.* Boston: Twayne Publisher, 1986.

Womack, John Jr. *Zapata and the Mexican Revolution.* New York: Vintage, 1968.

Zavala, Adriana. *Becoming Modern, Becoming Tradition: Women, Gender, and
Representations in Mexican Art.* University Park: Penn State University
Press, 2011.

INDEX

CPSIA information can be obtained
at www.ICGtesting.com
Printed in the USA
LVHW110553141222
735193LV00003B/10